Praise for *The Startup Lifecycle*

"*The Startup Lifecycle* communicates effectively Greg's impressive experience and unusual perspectives to create a book unlike what you see on shelves now. Whether you are a seasoned startup entrepreneur or interested, this book will make you really think! Greg's pragmatic advice distills decades of experience into a book I recommend for startup founders."

—**Dr. Michael K. Hawes, president and CEO of Fulbright Canada**

"I've never done a startup, but I've run a lot of organizations—from submarines and large staffs to the US Navy's 7th Fleet. In *The Startup Lifecycle*, Greg has brilliantly captured universal truths of leadership, planning, and management that are powerful for new organizations just getting started, but also very relevant for organizations of any size and age . . . particularly those that want to remain agile and avoid being disrupted. If I were still in uniform, *The Startup Lifecycle* would be required reading for everyone on my team."

—**Robert L. Thomas, Jr., ret. US Navy vice admiral**

"Greg's amazing experience and unusual perspectives make this book an incredibly powerful resource for startup entrepreneurs and even those who have been running enterprises for several years. The lessons he shares apply to practically any setting, including my own work in fostering localized economic research throughout the Global South. The book makes us rethink and organize in a structured and effective way our efforts to build our visions into full-fledged realizations."

—**John Cockburn, scientific advisor for Partnership for Economic Policy**

"*The Startup Lifecycle* communicates directly with founders and speaks to them in no-nonsense, concrete, and pragmatic language that expounds the lessons Shepard has learned, sometimes painfully, over his life, not just as an entrepreneur, but as a caring human being. This book is for any potential or practicing founder, no matter what your background is—all you need is the motivation to create a venture and the willingness to do the hard work needed to turn your idea into a successful and sellable company."

—**Amnon Dekel, PhD, executive director of ASPER-HUJI Innovate**

"Gregory Shepard offers a comprehensive guide with pragmatic advice to steer startups toward success. He distills decades of experience into seven clear phases, from vision to exit, enriched with insights from diverse experts. This book stands out for its actionable strategies, making it an essential resource for any entrepreneur aiming to defy the daunting startup failure rates. With its well-structured content, it promises a reliable road map for navigating the complex startup landscape."

—**Karl Swannie, CEO of Intlabs**

"*The Startup Lifecycle* is more than just a guide—it's an agent for change in fostering a diverse and inclusive startup ecosystem. This book not only teaches essential business strategies but also inspires founders to pursue their entrepreneurial visions with confidence and purpose. I highly recommend it to anyone dedicated to making an impactful and enduring mark in the business world."

—Lloyd Reshard, board chair at the Kukua Institute

"In *The Startup Lifecycle*, Greg Shepard delivers a masterclass in entrepreneurship, distilling decades of hard-won experience and invaluable insights into a comprehensive blueprint for startup success. Drawing on a wealth of real-world examples and interviews with diverse experts—from entrepreneurs to Navy SEALs—the book presents a road map that guides aspiring founders through every stage of building and selling a startup."

—Joyce Hunter, founder and president of
Data Science Camp Inc.

"Gregory Shepard's book, *The Startup Lifecycle*, is a must-read compendium for startups. This book is an empowering volume of resources that demystifies the concepts of startups in a remarkable way and provides a guide for every reader to embark on their entrepreneurial journey."

—Chika Chinwah, managing partner at
Entrepreneurship and Innovation Centre Ltd.

"What sets this book apart is its pragmatic approach, offering actionable strategies to navigate the treacherous waters of entrepreneurship and avoid common pitfalls that often lead to failure. Through seven meticulously outlined phases, from crafting the initial vision to achieving a lucrative exit, readers will gain a deep understanding of what it takes to build a sustainable and impactful business."

—Jan Smit, partner at ScaleUpNation Netherlands

"*The Startup Lifecycle* is an indispensable guide for any aspiring entrepreneur embarking on the exhilarating journey of building a startup. With a wealth of firsthand experience and insights gleaned from twelve successful exits, Greg Shepard delivers a comprehensive blueprint for navigating the treacherous waters of the startup world."

—Chris Massot, program director at the
Alacrity Foundation Canada

"With a focus on not only achieving financial success but also making a positive difference in the world, *The Startup Lifecycle* is a must-read for anyone embarking on the entrepreneurial journey. Whether you're a seasoned founder or a first-time entrepreneur, this book will equip you with the knowledge and tools needed to build a successful startup while leaving a lasting impact on society."

—Roberth Friedman, country manager for Sweden
at the Israel Ministry of Economy

"*The Startup Lifecycle* is an ethical guide for founders packed with key information yet explained in a manner which anyone can understand. Greg's down-to-earth explanations of complex patterns are unparalleled."

—Mike Wilkes, project manager at
McKinney Economic Development Corporation

"Greg Shepard offers a profound exploration of entrepreneurship in *The Startup Lifecycle*, leveraging years of firsthand experience to craft a definitive road map for startup success. Shepard provides an indispensable guide for aspiring founders, navigating them seamlessly through each pivotal phase of startup inception and eventual exit. This book deserves a place in every entrepreneurial educational program. Its insights could spare young entrepreneurs countless hours otherwise spent navigating the complexities of the startup journey."

—Jacques Chirazi, director of student entrepreneurship and
The Basement at the University of California San Diego

"*The Startup Lifecycle* has provided simple steps for any startup founder to work their way to success. I love how Greg breaks down different stages for consideration, which is easy to understand."

—Justin Ng, head of market growth at AngelHack

"Greg's entrepreneurial methodology is based on thirty years of experience, repeated successes, and his deep moral drive to improve well-being for everyone. His willingness to adapt to rapid change, learn from his failures, care for his team, and humbly pass on his knowledge are the same attributes found in successful combat leaders. Despite knowing and working with Greg for several years, I was still captured by this book—hooked and intrigued by his life experiences and how they translate into founder success. This is a must-read for new and experienced founders, and a necessary part of startup assistance programs."

—Lt. Col. Jeremy Gordon, ret. US Air Force pilot
and Distinguished Flying Cross recipient

THE
STARTUP
LIFECYCLE

THE
STARTUP
LIFECYCLE

The Definitive Guide to Building a Startup from Idea to Exit

GREGORY SHEPARD

BenBella Books, Inc.
Dallas, TX

BenBella Books, Inc.
10440 N. Central Expressway
Suite 800
Dallas, TX 75231
benbellabooks.com
Send feedback to feedback@benbellabooks.com

BenBella is a federally registered trademark.

Printed in the United States of America
10 9 8 7 6 5 4 3 2 1

Library of Congress Control Number: 2024010427
ISBN 9781637744321 (hardcover)
ISBN 9781637744338 (electronic)

Editing by Gregory Newton Brown
Copyediting by Michael Fedison
Proofreading by Rebecca Maines and Cape Cod Compositors, Inc.
Text design and composition by PerfecType, Nashville, TN
Cover design by Brigid Pearson
Cover image © Adobe Stock / Наталья Босяк
Printed by Lake Book Manufacturing

This book is dedicated to all those mentors and program managers who are committed to helping the founders that are evolving our world. The world appreciates you silently; the founders celebrate you aloud.

CONTENTS

INTRODUCTION

The test of our progress is not whether we add more to
the abundance of those who have much; it is whether
we provide enough for those who have too little.

–Franklin D. Roosevelt

W e are in trouble.
And no, I don't mean we as business owners. I mean we
as a world—really, we as *people* with hopes and aspirations for a better
world—are in *big* trouble.

According to data from the Federal Reserve (as of Q2 of 2022), the
top 1 percent of households in the United States held over 30 percent of
the country's wealth, while the bottom 50 percent of households had just
2.5 percent of the country's wealth. If you can visualize this, it should
hit home, because statistically speaking, the "less than" crowd and their
kids (and *their* kids) have a better chance of one day beating Usain Bolt
in a 100-meter sprint than becoming part of the elite 1 percent. This is
not just true in the United States. In fact, most of the world mirrors what

we see here. So many of us think that the rich are millionaires, or even those worth *hundreds of millions*, but the truth is that these people are worth much, *much* more. I'm talking numbers that most people can't even fathom.

This disparity becomes even more dire when you consider further reports from the Federal Reserve on wealth inequality through the lens of the racial wealth gap, indicating that "the average Black and Hispanic or Latino households earn about half as much as the average White household and own only about fifteen to twenty percent as much net wealth."

Why do I mention this? Well, if you're reading this book, there's a good chance that you are *not* part of that exorbitantly wealthy group. Some people, such as Elon Musk, Bill Gates, and Jeff Bezos, have achieved levels of income rarely, if ever, seen before . . . but most people won't even come close to moving beyond paycheck-to-paycheck living if things don't change! Let me say it more plainly: it's important for us to realize that the wealth inequality gap is *everywhere* in the world, and it's not just affecting marginalized groups of people (though they are often hit harder than other groups). The reality is that the wealth inequality gap includes *everyone*. The most frightening part of all of this is that the gap is widening.

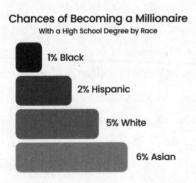

Chances of Becoming a Millionaire
With a High School Degree by Race

1% Black
2% Hispanic
5% White
6% Asian

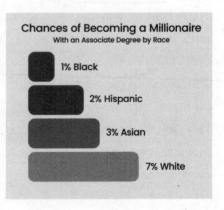

Chances of Becoming a Millionaire
With an Associate Degree by Race

1% Black
2% Hispanic
3% Asian
7% White

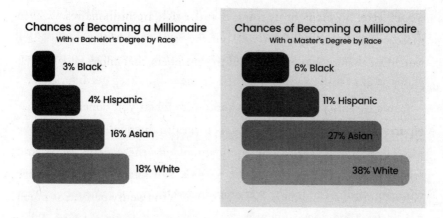

Chances of Becoming a Millionaire
With a Bachelor's Degree by Race

3% Black
4% Hispanic
16% Asian
18% White

Chances of Becoming a Millionaire
With a Master's Degree by Race

6% Black
11% Hispanic
27% Asian
38% White

To make matters worse, in recent years, we've seen financial devastation for people everywhere. The pandemic caused many people to lose their livelihoods, or entire businesses, as we entered the third recession in just two decades of the new century. The war in Ukraine has been costly,

Escaping Check to Check Living

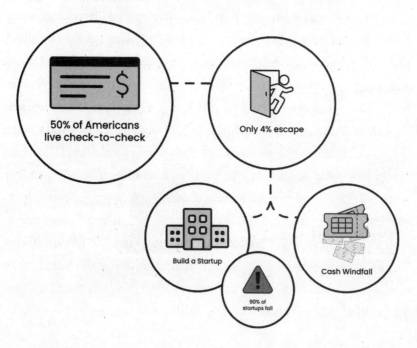

50% of Americans live check-to-check

Only 4% escape

Build a Startup

90% of startups fail

Cash Windfall

and inflation and the cost of living have skyrocketed, resulting in more and more Americans falling into the bottom 50 percent or remaining stagnant, living paycheck-to-paycheck, in fear of the next costly emergency. Meanwhile, the richest people in the nation keep getting richer.

But Let's Not Dwell on the Negatives

You probably purchased this book because you have an entrepreneurial curiosity within, reminding you often that working for someone else may not be the way to move up in the world. You may have already read books, articles, or blogs to determine whether you have what it takes to become an entrepreneur. I'm here as proof (you will read later) to tell you that somewhere within all of us is the drive and capacity to achieve greater things.

Why do people start a business? For one thing, there's greater autonomy, and more opportunities to utilize your own abilities, skills, and creativity. Plus, if you do it right, you can make a tremendous amount of money. But remember—and I say this quite often—money is an outcome, *not* a goal!

Of course, many people over the years have opened lifestyle businesses, from which (if done right) you and your family (perhaps even your grandchildren's families) can earn a very comfortable living. In the United States, and around the globe, there are businesses that have remained in families for decades. Consider, for example, the Kongō Gumi Co., Ltd., a Japanese construction company founded in AD 578, making it the world's oldest company. The business remained in the same family for the first 1,400 years!

In this book, however, I take a different route entirely. My goal is to teach you how to create and grow a startup by following a proven path that can lead to a successful sale of the business, or "exit," as we call it, with enough money and confidence to change your life forever. Today, thanks in large part to the proliferation of data, it is more feasible than ever before to launch a startup and sell it within five years for $2 million, $20 million, $200 million, or more. In this new age, multibillion-dollar conglomerates are steadily investing in and acquiring new businesses, as this is how innovation is done in the day of hyper-fast market movement, and we as a world have lots of problems to solve, which can result in opportunities to provide products and services, as well as to evolve and learn what is happening in the trenches.

Now you're probably thinking: *How in the world will I draw the attention of a major conglomerate with a startup?* And while this was once a seemingly insurmountable task, we have entered an era in which newer corporate giants, such as Google, Amazon, Apple, Meta, and even older companies, such as Unilever, General Motors, Cisco, and others, are not only buying startups, but are using startups for their research and development, as well as innovation. This is because new innovative startups have been passing up old corporations, and even putting them out of business, such as has been the case with many of the big box stores. Today, for the giants of business, it's not about being innovative . . . it's about *buying* innovation, and that's where your startup comes in. Companies want your new ways of seeing things, fresh ideas, new technology, and new products that can put them ahead of the competition. If ever there was a time to cash in on a major business deal, this is the time to start, by building a startup, growing it, and selling it. We'll return to selling your startup later in the book. In the meantime, use the knowledge that there are many buyers out there as motivation.

Your Startup Journey

I have no magic formula to sell you that will assure success, and no, this is not the equivalent of house flipping, and absolutely *not* a get-rich scheme. This is a tried-and-true—detailed—method of launching a startup business, following a series of specific steps, doing the work (e.g., plenty of research), and exiting with a successful sale. Does it always work? Nothing is guaranteed, but I have built and later sold twelve businesses for significant profits, many of which I talk about in stories throughout the upcoming chapters. And should you choose to make entrepreneurship a habit, or your life's work, as I did, you can replicate success.

While statistics correctly point out that many startups fail every year, my objective is to make sure your startup is not just one that doesn't *fail*, but also one that *succeeds* at building a business you can sell and enjoy a highly profitable exit.

Many of you may already be pondering some real startup business possibilities as you begin looking at this book with a twinkle in your eye and a vision in your heart, hoping to build something incredible with a bit of guidance along the way. And we'll get there, I promise! But first, I'd like to explain a bit about how I process the world and why I think that awareness of this data is vital to your journey.

Put simply: data is how I process the world around me.

The Weird Kid

Growing up, I was the "weird kid." At the time, my undiagnosed "weird" issues made me a favorite of bullies, who teased, taunted, or beat me up on a daily basis . . . it was like making my life miserable was on their daily to-do list.

I knew I was very different from other kids, but not until years later was I diagnosed with synesthesia, savant syndrome, severe dyslexia, and autism (ADOS Level 1), which, according to the medical community, is not a processing disorder, but a totally different operating system.

While I was bullied and ostracized for most of my life due to my neurodivergence, the advantage these bullies gave me was life-changing grit and an understanding of how I could see the world differently. I learned to stop fighting against the way I was hardwired and gained the ability to process information in a unique way. Where many neurotypical individuals see numbers that reflect inevitable doom and gloom, I see patterns and places for opportunity; I see a bigger picture that's just waiting to be painted. This unique perspective has played a role in what has led me to the success I have achieved today and why I believe that, despite the current failure rates among startups, success is within reach for people of all walks of life. The doom and gloom we face today isn't the be-all, end-all. It's a symptom of deeply rooted issues that we need to work hard to fix.

I'll continue sharing my personal story with you throughout this book, detailing many of my trials, tribulations, and victories. However, I feel it's incredibly important to highlight that, despite all the difficulties I faced with my neurodivergence in a world built for neurotypicals, growing up under the poverty line, and facing bullying from peers and authority figures alike, I found a way to succeed—not once, not twice, not even three times, but twelve times! After one success, I was able to reinvest that wealth in other startups with revolutionary ideas, and now I am trying my best, any way I can, to contribute to our ever-evolving world. If I can do it, you can too.

It's a New Dawn

Consider that we are at the precipice of a new frontier. We are moving into an age in which startup businesses can be carefully constructed with an exit strategy in mind from the start. Maybe this doesn't erase *all* that's wrong in our world, but I hope that sharing my road map to success is a pivotal piece of the greater puzzle that will help you start achieving success and building a better world with your incredible ideas. I truly believe that startups are a means to recognizing and encouraging such achievement, while playing a part in repairing the wealth inequality that is tearing our world apart.

As I mentioned earlier, I'm a big-picture thinker. I know that one book won't fix the whole system. But, as my mom used to say, "If you think because you're small you don't matter, then you have never spent a night in a tent with a mosquito."

Ultimately, I think that we need to turn toward a model of altruistic capitalism, which is to say, leveraging our powerful capitalist system for altruistic outcomes, a model where bold new perspectives are invited to the table and underserved, marginalized communities are recognized for their ambitious inventions and innovations that will make our country (and our world) a better, more sustainable place. I believe that the most challenging problems need to be solved by those experiencing them (aka subject matter experts, or SMEs for short) and the startup ecosystem, which is essentially the startup universe, including all the people involved (from advisors to customers) to the infrastructure, products, processes, legislation, and everything that pertains to a startup.

It is important that those of us who have succeeded as founders foster these brave people who take on the challenge of starting a new business. We must help them incubate their ideas, set them up for success, and celebrate them, much like we celebrate military people. And the way we should also recognize and celebrate teachers. When that success is reached, these founders can then take their newly acquired wealth and invest it in their communities and the next wave of founders within these communities.

It Starts with Education

When I say "education," I don't necessarily mean *formal* education. I recently did a study of innovation and entrepreneur programs, only to find that a *fraction of a percent* of those traditional instructors, the people guiding the founders of tomorrow, have ever built a startup themselves or even worked at one. *I was floored.* While I'm not here to tell folks to throw formal education by the wayside, it's clear that we need *experienced* people teaching, as in those who have been through the gauntlet and survived.

Many of history's greatest "teachers" did not just follow a linear path built around lessons learned in books and classrooms but were educated largely from lessons learned in life. We need to respect experience, *real* experience, as education. You can study how to ride a bike and watch other people ride a bike, but that doesn't mean you can or should be teaching others to. I have the most respect for teachers. My mother, who was a teacher for thirty years, told me, "Part of being a teacher is understanding your power and limitations."

We also need standardization so people can communicate more easily and learn the best practices for startups. Most importantly, we need *free* access to these materials, which means stopping the gatekeepers from locking so many of us out of the opportunity to get our startup from that twinkle in our eye to an exit that will allow us to move away from paycheck-to-paycheck living once and for all.

Entrepreneurship is the future, and it needs to be accessible to everyone. We need to give the map to success to those people who are traditionally shut out. It's my hope that this book will be that map.

Above, I mentioned that more subject matter experts need to be given space to solve issues they deal with every day. It's understandable that you may still be left wondering what that means! So, I'd like to take a brief pit stop at this topic before we dive into the nitty-gritty of the Startup Science Lifecycle.

Believe me, if you look at enough startup concepts, the mystery as to what makes a successful one becomes a little clearer, as patterns begin to emerge. Such patterns also help when moving into investing. I've spoken to literally thousands of founders. As a result, I've noticed that successful founders typically fall into one of two categories: they're either visionaries or subject matter experts.

- **A visionary** is someone who generates ideas by approaching problems from the outside in. They start out with a new way of thinking, or a new way of doing something, and then apply it to an existing problem to generate value. In other words, they start with a hammer and go looking for nails to whack. Someone like the legendary Steve Jobs is the archetypal startup visionary. He transformed established industries by bringing in his own unique blend of tech prowess and marketing genius. Visionaries see a manner in which something, such as using a computer or traveling by automobile, can be innovated into something revolutionary. Henry Ford, for example, did not invent the automobile. He made it better, easier to assemble, and more affordable for the masses. Likewise, Steve Jobs did not invent the computer, but he had the vision to put a computer in the hands of everyone.

- **A subject matter expert (SME)** is someone who, on the other hand, approaches problems from the inside out. They're already immersed in their field and leverage that expertise to identify and solve unaddressed challenges. Alongside visionary Steve Jobs was Steve Wozniak, the subject matter expert. Teaming up with visionary Bill Gates was Paul Allen, the subject matter expert. The visionary is more of the "renaissance" person looking at the broad picture, while the subject matter expert is deeply involved in a specific area of expertise. They work on the nuts and bolts of the visionary's plan. There's a great book on the topic called *Rocket Fuel* by Gino Wickman and Mark C. Winters, which talks about visionaries and implementers, which I refer to as subject matter experts (SMEs) in the context of founders. I have worked with a number of SMEs who became founders. In one success story, a veteran in the government space created a successful platform for government legislative drafting. Another example entailed helping an SME sell a transportation technology platform developed from a founder who had years of expertise in the transportation sector. Founders can be either visionaries or SMEs, and on occasion, both. Often, founders consist of a partnership between a visionary and a subject matter expert, as noted in the examples above.

I've tried both approaches when working on various startups over the years. My biggest successes came as a subject matter expert in the digital marketing space—a sector I helped to define, which I will talk more about in chapter one. I've also taken the plunge into industries in which I was *un*familiar. In the applied environmental biotechnology space, I researched, engaged with, and hassled with a mentor, Dr. Howard Warren. He had created a truly revolutionary bioremediation technology that addressed the root cause of clogged filters and pipes from public wastewater. While this does not sound sexy in the slightest, it is a "substantial problem," which is another phrase for "substantial opportunity." Dr. Warren lacked the vision to see how to create a startup around his invention. So, armed with Dr. Warren's guidance and blessing, I leveraged his invention to build an environmental biotechnology startup that was eventually acquired by a publicly traded Canadian company. In this example, he was the expert, and I was the visionary.

When you think of your startup vision, with that twinkle in your eye, what kind of founder do you see yourself being? How have your past business and personal experiences shaped the entrepreneurial path you want to take? Often, this comes in the form of problems that you have encountered personally and have ideas of how to resolve.

I've Done the Research

Don't worry, I do recognize that entrepreneurship is a little scary. Sometimes a lot scary. I'll dive deeper into the numbers in the next chapter, but most observers know enough to be nervous about the "doomed to fail" reputation startups have garnered over time. I'm not here to convince you that this isn't the truth. The unfortunate reality is that startups got this reputation because it *is* true. Failure is more common than success, and that failure is nothing to ignore when weighing the risks of your livelihood with the small possibility of striking gold in a successful exit.

Therefore, the question isn't "How do you become the rare one of the few to beat the odds?" It's not that we expect to use startups to heal what's broken in our society and economy. No, our question needs to be "How do *we* fix the failure rate so *everyone* has a real, even a *likely*, chance at success?" And the follow-up to that isn't just a matter of why startups fail, but rather *why*, *when*, and *how*.

These are, admittedly, questions that I have been asking for a long time and ones that I'm hoping to answer with this book and any future books I write. Aside from my own personal journey, I've conducted years of research and thousands of one-to-one interviews with people ranging from wildly successful serial entrepreneurs and investors to Air Force fighter pilots who process immense amounts of information and remain calm to Navy SEALs who specialize in strategy, grit, and perseverance through grueling challenges.

Why I Wrote This Book

I watched my parents struggle to provide for a large family, which was made up of non-biological children and biological children that didn't fit any mold, like me and my neurodivergent challenges.

I remember feeling hungry.

I remember feeling stupid.

I remember feeling like I didn't belong.

I also remember how it felt *every time* one of my ideas put money in my pocket.

Being able to contribute to our family has had the most lasting impact on my life. It is that feeling I want to give to founders as part of the gratitude I feel for achieving what I have with the ability to pay it forward. I've come a long way from being a bullied, scrawny, autistic kid who had to wait until the hen laid an egg to have breakfast. I want to share some of my most pertinent stories and practical findings, in the hope that they will help other founders to achieve their dreams and change their own destinies and all of ours for the better.

Therefore, I wrote this book for two reasons. The first is because of the massive income inequality issue, especially for people of color, and the

Hispanic and LGBTQIA+ communities, who continue to struggle. The neurodivergent and disabled community are at the bottom of the list, with virtually no chance of moving up unless they are born into wealth.

When I was young, I would make a habit of meeting people who seemed successful. One of them said, "Greg, you have a better chance of getting hit by lightning in your home than becoming successful," and he was actually pretty close. As a society, we're just sweeping our marginalized communities under the rug when it comes to income inequality. That's not acceptable. As human beings, we all deserve that chance of life, liberty, and the pursuit of happiness, which is realistically unattainable for so many people. I want to be a part of the solution.

The way I see it, I can contribute to solving the income inequality issue by helping to create empowered, well-educated founders of any race, gender, economic background, or education level, by teaching them how to conceptualize a startup with a winning product and drive it through the Startup Science Lifecycle, which is a proven path to success. From experiences, both good and bad, I know for sure that every business idea must go through a specific lifecycle to become "beg-worthy" to investors. It's a big promise, but one I have seen fulfilled for people repeatedly. I've seen people learn how to successfully raise seed money, and then drive an exit at the right time.

The second reason I wrote this book is to give current and future founders everywhere a fighting chance to achieve financial independence and the ability to drive the future. In particular, this book is designed to help guide those who may feel as though they don't belong in the founder community. Rest assured, *you belong here*. Foundership is more than just fancy offices in Silicon Valley. It means solving a problem that is important to you and your community, and the world.

One change in the global system is that, thanks to free online learning and shorter specialty school programs, a college degree is slowly getting devalued in many areas of business. There are even venture firms who favor investing in Stanford dropouts! While I'm not saying college is a detriment, the reality is that you no longer need a fancy degree from an Ivy League school to work in tech. You just need to know how to code. You don't need gatekeeper approval to start a podcast or YouTube channel in your area of expertise. You just need to learn video and audio editing and your way around the necessary equipment—a hands-on process. Creating a system that everyone can follow helps achieve this big goal! While pharma and other startups require this academia, most startups just need deep experience and "a handful" of things—five things to be specific— focus, drive, enthusiasm, discipline, and optimism.

Things are changing, and the path to success is widening. Recent research has seen a noticeable drop in traditional degrees and an even larger increase in entrepreneurship. Partly due to the amount of data available online, we are witnessing, perhaps, the most fundamental disruption of the Internet, the age of the autodidact (self-taught). This is eroding the barriers to foundership, which are being bypassed by innovative and determined founders. Yes, the day and the age of startup success is upon us. What gets me out of bed in the morning is the abundance of opportunity for historically marginalized groups: BIPOC, women, LGBTQIA+, as well as neurodivergent and disabled people. Whether you fit into one of these groups or several, and experience the hardships that come with them, you deserve, at minimum, a fighting chance!

It's a privilege and an honor to guide you on your founder's journey, and I can't wait to see what you build. Let's get to work!

How to Navigate This Book

This book is split into two parts. In Part One, I take you on a brief journey through some of my early startups and the lessons I've learned along the way. Then we'll move into what's wrong with many startups today and the reasons why so many fail.

In Part Two, I will explain the seven phases of the Startup Science Lifecycle from finding your North Star and vision to producing a product prototype, taking it to market, standardizing and optimizing it, to growing and scaling your startup . . . and finally, moving to selling your business and forever changing your life, through a "successful exit." Believe me, it's not as easy as it sounds. In fact, it's a lot of hard work and requires perseverance and grit, but the results make it all worthwhile.

Throughout the chapters, I've also incorporated my experience and knowledge, including what I learned from my own failures and missteps, into the development of this system and into this book, to help founders avoid these unnecessary pains and lagging indicators that lead to startup failure. By giving founders the proper tools and warning signs to stay on track, we can also help you, as a founder, achieve a reasonable timeline from vision to exit—in approximately three to five years! And, if you decide to hold onto the business longer, that's fine, too—as long as you do not become one of the failed startups.

Ultimately, I want to provide a system that creates mutual understanding of what success looks like at different points and guide founders on the best practices for tracking, communicating, and forecasting progress. In other words, a system that helps ensure entrepreneurs and investors are speaking the same language, which leads to greater synergy and success, and I want to share it with as many people as I can.

The key insight that most investors have, and that many new founders lack, is that every startup is born, grows, and matures in a predictable way, or, as I noted earlier, every startup follows the same basic lifecycle. I'll remind you of this again later on.

As for me, I dream of a future where a startup becomes the answer to building generational wealth for anyone who, as Colin Wilson said, "desires change more than the desire to stay the same." To go along with that idea, I must point out the contribution of Dan Millman, a world-class gymnast who, in 1980, released the first edition of *Way of the Peaceful*

Warrior. His book was a fictionalized memoir that explored the physical and mental challenges Millman faced in his early life and the spiritual growth he experienced. In this book, he wrote, "The secret of change is to focus all of your energy, not on fighting the old, but on building the new." Writing this book is one of the ways I can contribute to this dream of creating a better future for entrepreneurs.

Remember, anything is possible.

As a child I grew up in a paycheck-to-paycheck family, and many years later I met the president of the United States, Barack Obama.

Note: I was not able to fit all of the information I hoped for in this book, so at the end of each chapter, you'll find a QR code that links to free micro-learning classes, resources, and tools related to each chapter to fur-
ther introduce you to the startup ecosystem, starting with this one to provide you with more context as you begin your startup journey. I truly hope you find every- thing you need and if not please let me know and I'll add it. I hope to hear from you, and enjoy the journey.

Laying the Foundation for Startups

Rattlesnake Salesman to Startup Guru

Look closely at the present you are constructing: it should look like the future you are dreaming of.

–Alice Walker, Pulitzer Prize-winning author

As you may have ascertained, being "the weird kid" evolved into being a unique author. I differ from many authors who pen business books in several ways. For starters, I did not go to an Ivy League university. In fact, I never went to a university at all, nor a fancy business school, for that matter. The truth is, I barely graduated from high school.

Now you might wonder how, with autism, synesthesia, and severe dyslexia—which makes reading and writing difficult, to say the least—I was able to succeed repeatedly as an entrepreneur, much less write a book about it. While it has always been quite a challenging set of circumstances,

I now believe that my neurodivergent conditions are a gift—all of them. Getting bullied every day was certainly not a gift, but even that made me stronger and raised my mental and physical threshold.

Despite all my personal academic challenges, today I teach foundership at universities around the world. I have done a TEDx Talk (if you wish to watch it—which would be cool—you'll find it at the QR code at the end of this chapter). I have even received an honorary degree from a university that I could never have dreamed of getting into. So, clearly, there's a twist to my story, which began with a nun and a priest falling in love, leaving the church, and moving to California to raise a family.

I grew up in a chaotic, crowded household, along with a motley crew of siblings. While my family—or tribe, as we called it—had love, we did not have much money. Still, I've always admired my parents' willingness to take chances, pursue their dreams, make mistakes, and build a new life. My mother became a special education teacher and my stepfather an emergency room nurse's assistant. Unfortunately, there isn't much money in teaching or nursing (at least not enough to support a family the size of ours). Despite the fact that these are incredibly valuable lines of work, as you may know, they are extremely underpaid.

We grew up in a rough part of the California Bay Area. To protect us, my mom moved us to an inexpensive but beautiful patch of land in a mountain town southwest of Lake Tahoe. The only challenge we faced was that there was no house on the land. So, we spent the first two years living in tents, while my brother, uncle, mom, and I built the first half of what eventually became a house. Our clothes were all hand-me-downs, and we constantly smelled of campfires. It was such a great experience, but not a good thing for a special-ed kid at school. It was a hard time, and we were literally living paycheck-to-paycheck.

We would eat what we grew or raised and only went to the store for nonperishable items. I still remember standing around the chicken coop on many a cold morning, waiting for the hen to lay an egg, then grabbing the steaming egg out of the coop to cook on the wood stove for break-fast. It's tempting to romanticize this kind of struggle. The reality is that, while Walden Pond was fine for Thoreau, there's nothing romantic about a hungry teenager staring at the business end of a chicken waiting for it to deliver breakfast.

My life at school was truly awful. My grandfather used to say, "Greg will end up either rich or in jail," and my mom would always comfort me with the wise words, "When you're going through hell, keep going." I remember overhearing two teachers actually say, "Give him a coloring book. It's not like he'll change the world." Fortunately, I was also told, "Learn to work hard. You can always rely on hard work. It doesn't take an education."

So, I worked hard.

Opportunities Are Everywhere: Notice Them, Then Strike

While school may have been a huge struggle for me, hard work turned out to be easy. I would wake up early, feed the livestock (which gave me one of my first startup ideas), ride my bike ten miles to Conway Ranch to work on their irrigation systems, change clothes in the barn, and get the bus to school. After school, I would do the whole thing again, finishing up around dinner (if there was any left). I also did construction work on the weekends and throughout the summer.

While doing the hard, physical work of laying irrigation systems or working construction, my mind would swirl with all kinds of ideas that didn't always seem connected. The physical labor, no matter how hot and sweaty, gave me time to just think in solitude about the things I observed in the world. My particular "weirdness" did not deprive me of a burning desire to be more, to have more, and to help out my family. I now see those days, when my body did the hard work and my mind flitted from idea to idea, as the first spark of the entrepreneurial flame that has defined my life. Wherever I saw a problem, I would figure out how I could solve it. I would hear people say "somebody should make that" and realize people want, need, and buy things that solve problems.

One of my "side hustles" was selling pork "futures" to my neighbors—getting people to pay in advance for meat, then using their money to buy and raise piglets. We'd have one hog left over at the end of the season, and that would wind up in our bellies. Eggs *and* bacon for breakfast?! I was moving up in the world!

Although my peculiar neural operating system has caused me no small measure of pain and hardship, it has also endowed me with some invaluable gifts. I have an uncanny ability to discern patterns and a prodigious capacity to conceptualize systems. My autism can be a nightmare, but my divergent neural operating system has paid off over time.

From an early age, I have used this atypical skill set to build businesses. As a "weird kid," I always had one crazy business idea after the other. As an adult, I've built (or helped build) and sold other people's not-so-crazy business ideas.

This has led me to my current life's work: helping entrepreneurs succeed. Being that I am wired to see patterns, over and over, I've used this capability to observe the same patterns governing success and failure.

My Early Startup Days

Besides providing for my family, these "startup ideas" proved to me that I wasn't as stupid as I was told. Albert Einstein, a fellow neurodivergent, observed, "Everybody is a genius, but if you judge a fish by its ability to climb a tree, it will spend its whole life believing that it is stupid."

It became clear to me that, if I were to be more and have more, I wouldn't get there by listening to what people told me was not possible.

Instead, it would require that I trust my own way of thinking, which I had yet to fully understand. Instinctively, I embraced my seemingly disconnected thoughts rather than fighting against them. I knew that if I didn't take matters into my own hands, I'd amount to nothing, as people kept telling me.

Raising pigs was all well and good, but I also wanted to put some money in my pocket, so I diversified—and started catching rattlesnakes. I'd get a long, still-green, fresh stick, split one end, and put a twig in between to keep it open. Then I'd head out into the hills until I found a rattler basking among the rocks, and I'd stab my split stick over its neck without hurting it, pinning it in place until I could bundle it—more or less safely—into a livestock feed sack. There was a guy in town who would milk the rattlers I brought him for antivenin production, then cut the fangs and sell them to herpetologists and reptile collectors. I'd get a couple hundred bucks per rattlesnake—big money for a teenager back in the eighties!

Of course, the boom didn't last forever. You see, while I had the inventory acquisition and sales side of things down pat, my "warehouse" wasn't much to speak of. After making my way home with a bag full of snakes, I would sneak down to the lowest section of our basement and pour them out of the feed sacks into a cage. I was lucky that they never broke out, but—in that relief—I forgot that when you put a bunch of scared rattlers in a cage, they're going to make *noise*. My mom came home and walked around on the floor above, and the rattlers would go off like a drum roll. It didn't take long for my mom to notice the alarm they were sounding. Fearing an infestation under the house, she called in an animal control officer, who busted my entire operation. As soon as he let her know that he had found the rattlers conveniently contained in a cage in the basement, she knew it was me, and well, let's say that was the end of my first business venture. It was devastating! I wasn't thinking about all the ways those rattlesnakes could bust out of the cage. I was a silly teenager who had just lost a lot of money after investing my time catching a bunch of snakes for my lucrative little business. My business was certain to die if I couldn't catch and keep any more snakes. The jig was up . . . *for now.*

My First Pivot

I burrowed into the problem with that now-familiar intensity. If I could no longer sell snakes, what could I do without having to completely start over? In what I would later call the "Rattlesnake Strategy," I asked my snake buyer what the pet stores and collectors needed to take care of the reptiles.

"They feed them rats, mostly," he replied.

The next day, I went out and bought myself a couple of rats—one male, one female—and started up a breeding operation to supply my contact. In the startup world, this is called a pivot! My mom wasn't thrilled with my chosen pivot, but she figured it was better than having me get bitten by rattlesnakes!

In our small California gold rush town, there was a plaque proclaiming, "The German immigrant Levi Strauss made his fortune here." Levi then moved to San Francisco, where the brand took off. It was in this town that my mom gave me the best business advice I have ever received. She said, "The people mining for gold are not the winners. It's those who sell them the Levi's who win." That's what I did with this situation. I was not the gold miner catching the snakes anymore; I was Levi selling the food for the snakes.

This single piece of advice forever changed the way I looked at making money. I began to focus on the ideas in my head in a totally different way.

Welcome to My Mind; Don't Go There Alone!

As a result of my neurological differences, the way my mind works is to find patterns and create systems that I can understand and optimize.

Where other people see disconnected dots, which can feel overwhelming and unrelated to them, my mind connects the dots to find patterns. Pretty much everything I see creates a pattern in my mind! While it can be tiresome, and sometimes I want to just shut it down, I use those patterns to create systems to understand what they mean and how to use them. If I were to draw a visual representation of how my mind works, it would look like the image on the right.

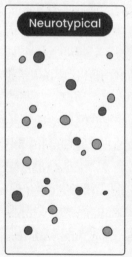 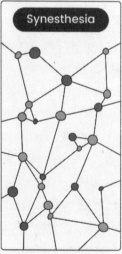

I have systems for just about everything in my life, from shaving to working, to how to greet people and end conversations. While these systems get me through social anxiety situations, they also apply to business ideas and execution.

Basically, a neurotypical person sees individual pieces of data, silos of data. Most look at something, like the solar system, the sun, and the earth, as individual, disconnected entities. I see everything all connected, all the time, entangled and related. The individual pieces are not separate; they are a pattern. I see them as a picture or a Newton's Cradle, where they are all connected and affecting one another, not individual entities. This is the world to me all the time. I used to hate it, but I have learned to love it!

In startups, some see advisors, investors, customers, vendors, and entrepreneurs, but I see it as an entangled ecosystem, directly. As a result of my neurological differences, the way my mind works, the way I survive is by finding patterns and creating systems.

People have told me that they also see patterns. The difference is when I say "see," I literally *see* these things as shapes and feel their colors as emotions. Welcome to synesthesia. This type of thinking also contributed to one of my biggest fears, thalassophobia, or the fear of deep water. I've overcome my fear by taking part in an annual challenge to swim a 10K in open water. Many people think of the ocean (for example) as water, or animals, or seaweed, or sand—all little parts that coexist in a space together. I see the ocean as all of those things at once, which is freaky, and makes me feel like an invader swimming in someone else's body. During my time confronting this fear, I've taken moments during every swim to thank the water for letting me be there as a part of its wide and complex ecosystem.

The Rattlesnake Strategy

It's been the same story ever since: I've always had an eye for opportunities, and a willingness to throw myself into the deep end, figure things out, and turn opportunities into real moneymaking enterprises, my neurological quirks lighting the way. Moving on from pork futures, rats, and rattlesnakes, I became a break-dancer for donations, sold Rubik's Cubes, Christmas mistletoe, and just about anything else I thought people would buy.

Despite my several business endeavors, thinking I had limited options, I joined the Navy. My mom was extremely upset. She said, "Greg, you are the artist of your life. Why would you give the paintbrush to someone else?" In any case, that did not last long. I was kicked out for omitting any mention of my asthma and autism (I hid the former and was ignorant of the latter). With $133.77 in my pocket, I took a commissioned sales job that offered skills I knew I needed: computer skills and an understanding of finance. I sold everything from computer learning to mortgages and took all the free classes on computer sciences and technology that were offered. Then, I took a sales job at a mortgage lender to learn what I thought was finance, again taking all the classes. Thinking, *I'm ready*, I started a bungee jumping business, a mortgage lending business, and eventually, I moved up to applied environmental biotechnologies.

Although I was growing to accept that fighting my brain was my least lucrative option, I was still working to nail down the places where disconnects existed. I needed a strategy that built on the Levi Strauss lesson I learned as a kid: if you can't sell the rattlesnakes, you start selling everything that snake lovers need to keep them alive. That's where I distilled the fundamental steps of the Rattlesnake Strategy, which says that you need to:

1. Understand your ecosystem (startup universe).
2. Look for the problems: What is missing, being overlooked, or could be done in a more effective/efficient manner?
3. Find the opportunities, like frustrations, limitations, needs, wants, and pain points. Then ask yourself: What can I do to alleviate such problems?

I looked around me and remembered my mom's lesson about Levi Strauss. I started to notice the opportunity that lived in all the places that others weren't able to see. Soon, selling rats to snake lovers and jeans to gold miners became a pertinent thought model. Any disruption begets opportunities. In fact, it presents far more opportunities than the disruption itself. In today's world, there are even startups created to help startups, making the startups the miners and those that service them the Levi's.

The Rattlesnake Strategy facilitates the discovery of where the *real* opportunity lies. At the end of the day, a miner may strike gold and get rich or work all day in the muck only to find nothing, and a company may close an extraordinary deal or lose a landmark client. All miners need tools to enable their success and companies need tools to land clients and close successful deals. Patterns are everywhere; seeing them is the art I cannot teach, but I can teach the science behind finding and utilizing such patterns.

Disrupting the Performance Marketing Industry

Most of my ventures did well, but none better than Affiliate Traction. It turned out to be a wildly successful digital venture that disrupted and helped define the fledgling affiliate marketing space at a time when everyone was still trying to figure out how to reach customers online. In the early days of the Internet, I learned the basics of coding and built startups, while selling police bicycle lights, magazine subscriptions, and travel products, like travel insurance, passports, visas, and foreign currency.

After the gold rush of building websites tapered off, customers needed to know how to draw people to their sites. I had many customers saying things like, "Okay, now I have a website, but nobody knows it exists," or "It's like having a store in the middle of the desert." *Boom!* An idea. Listening to their concerns, I created a means of marketing so people could draw traffic to their websites. Over the course of seventeen years, I became a true vertical subject matter expert and thought leader in what was a new disruption industry . . . affiliate marketing.

I solidified my position in the industry through thought leadership, like keynotes, panels, and published articles, which culminated in a clean, all-cash exit.

I had successfully pivoted from providing websites to enabling online advertising and finally to *affiliate marketing*—an advertising model in which a company compensates partners who use *their* web channels to drive online traffic to the company's products and services, resulting in sales. I saw growth in affiliate marketing as inevitable.

The Dotcom Era, the Dotcom Bomb, and the 2008 Crash

Over that rough-and-tumble seventeen-year spell, I built Affiliate Traction up into an industry leader—the first agency to go worldwide—despite almost losing everything twice, during the dotcom bomb in 2000, and again during the 2008 crash. After each setback, I persevered and rebuilt. Then, in 2016, I sold the startup to eBay Enterprise Marketing Solutions as part of a $925M transaction that included digital marketing pioneer Pepperjam and the e-commerce giant Magento, both later sold to Partnerize and Adobe, respectively. The deal won four private equity industry awards in the $250M to $1B transaction category.

Once the transaction was complete, I was asked to develop a technical, operational, and product vision across the now much larger combined startup as chief strategy officer, then later to execute the strategy in the role of chief technology officer. After the technology was built, the go-to-market (GTM) plan was implemented to great success as the new combined company sold again to Partnerize, a partnership management solution platform.

After three years, I was able to step down to focus once again on what I love: building startups. Clear of all prior commitments, I could finally start to give back. I initially sought out politics, working as a chairman for a congressional candidate, but I was left disenchanted by the political system's operational playbook. I found myself looking for another way to give back. I've since started an investment syndicate (a group of like-minded investors) and launched a founderial education and software startup targeting corporations, investors, and startup assistance programs (SAPs), like incubators and accelerators. Both of these support the early-phase startup ecosystem in their own way, and are ultimately focused on dropping the proverbial 90 percent startup failure rate.

CHAPTER WRAP-UP

The objective of telling my story in this opening chapter is not to boast or sing my own praises, but to illustrate how this journey worked for me. My hope is that you, as a founder, learn from the highs and lows of my arduous journey. My goal is simply to give more people the opportunity to defy the odds and succeed in building a successful startup and selling it to the right acquirer at the right time.

The Problem with Silicon Valley Thinking

Obviously there are positives to working in the epicen-
ter of innovation. But there are also disadvantages.

**—Peter Barris, Founding Venture Capital
Investor in Groupon**

There is perhaps no place more associated with foundership and
society-changing innovation than Silicon Valley. In the past few
decades, Silicon Valley has become, to founders of startups, what Hollywood has long been to aspiring actors. It's a place where dreams can come
true. Founders of all sorts come to Silicon Valley, dreaming about how
they will "make an exit." Of course, there's a catch. Silicon Valley might
be a place where dreams come true, but—like Hollywood—it is not a

place where everyone's dreams come true. For every Google, Apple, or Meta, there are countless startups that fall by the wayside and thousands of smart, hardworking founders with great ideas who wind up with more regrets than riches.

Silicon Valley's Dirty Secret

Founders face many hurdles when it comes to building a startup that is viewed as investment worthy. Silicon Valley's dirty secret is that their definition of success is very narrow: unicorn, decacorn, hectocorn . . . or bust. The narrow definition, as promulgated primarily by venture capitalists, makes sense for investors: they'll reap a bigger return from backing one unicorn than from getting behind a dozen smaller startups, so they're happy to set sky-high goals, even if it means most of the startups that they back will wind up failing as a result. Investors understand and budget for that failure. They're playing the long game, and they know, expect, and accept that most of the founders they back *will* ultimately fail. Essentially, it's the theory that, if you back thirty companies knowing that one will likely become a massive success, covering your gamble on the twenty-nine that fail, you'll be coming out ahead . . . but at the expense of twenty-nine failed founders. To me, it just seems lazy. It's taking the easy way, and there is, for sure, a better way!

Redefining the Mythical Unicorn

FYI: The term "unicorn" was coined in 2013 by Aileen Lee, founder of Cowboy Ventures, a seed-phase venture capital firm. She named a startup valued at US $1 billion a "unicorn." A startup valued at more than US $10 billion is a "decacorn." A startup valued at over US $100 billion is a "hectocorn."

As you start focusing attention on building your startup, you will find investors that support early-phase, growth-driven companies for a fixed period of time, through education, mentorship, and financing. These are known as "accelerators" and "incubators," which are similar in that they are focused on coaching and developing startups so they can secure early-phase "pre-seed" and "seed" funding. They also provide a range of assistance and support services to startups. Both accelerators and incubators prefer to work with for-profit startups with high-growth potential.

Startups typically enter as part of a cohort of companies and move through the accelerator experience, which is a process of intense, rapid, and immersive education aimed at accelerating the lifecycle of young, innovative companies, compressing years' worth of learning-by-doing into just a few months. Accelerators, incubators, and early-phase angel investors often—but not always—take a "spray-and-pray" approach to investing, accepting that just a few of the startups they back will ultimately take flight. Later-phase investors have less tolerance for risk, but still, know that not all the startups in their portfolios will succeed. Most understand and require investors to also understand that there is a huge risk. This does not need to be the case. In fact, I believe this mindset is part of the problem itself. You, as a founder, understand that you are the captain of the vessel, and no one cares as much as you do, nor can anyone make success happen the way that you can. Do not for a minute think anyone has your back or as much to lose as you do. You will get help, for sure, but the outcome is on you, full stop. But, on the other hand, don't let fear of failure become your future. Failure is a lesson learned and success is that lesson applied!

Incubators and accelerators can be beneficial by providing research and support that can help you move forward more quickly on your journey. They can provide a place for learning from professionals who've been there / done that, and also networking with other founders. However, you need to be careful that you don't lose control of your startup or give up too much of your future profits. In other words, talk to and learn from others about their experience with an accelerator or incubator before you get involved.

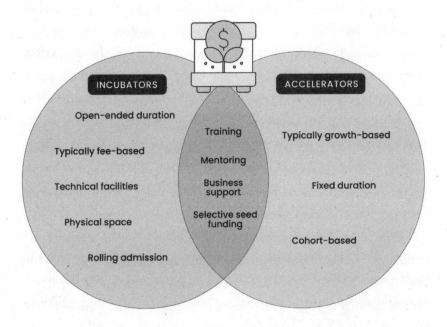

The Capital Trap

It is important to consider what taking on investment money can mean as you build a startup with the goal of achieving an exit. As a founder, your goal isn't to help your investors meet their quota of unicorns; it's to make your own startup the best it can be and to make smart decisions about the risk you're taking on.

When you position yourself as a unicorn to investors, you're locking yourself into a trajectory that requires raising large amounts of capital, growing incredibly fast, and satisfying an ever-growing array of benchmarks and metrics issued by investors who are *only* interested in your potential for delivering an enormous return on *their* investment, again to offset all the losses and their extremely high operating costs. These

Silicon Valley–style startups must always be in "hyper growth," which is equivalent to trying to ride a skateboard at thirty miles per hour. You might make it on smooth asphalt, but good luck if you hit a pebble! There is a high probability you will lose control of your startup and your destiny through no fault of your own, for no founder's journey occurs without hitting pebbles, let alone boulders, strewn across the road. The perfect assent from startup to exit is a bumpy road, but well worth the journey. In this case, when you hit the proverbial bump in the road, Silicon Valley investors are not going to help you get back on your feet. They will be too busy looking for the next skateboarder to come along.

Too many founders fall into a capital trap, where they get lost in the maze due to the speed and pressure to achieve valuations demanded by investors. When I first started to understand this problem, it bothered me greatly. So many good people with incredible dreams for startups that would change the course of their family's life—or perhaps even the world—are shattered by an ecosystem that was meant to help them succeed. It bothered me so much that I decided to try and fix the problem by going on a mission to understand more.

Many Years, $500K, and 1,200 Interviews Later

Startups are generally privately held and funded, meaning they have no obligation to disclose information about their successes and failures. To pierce this opacity, I ended up conducting over 1,200 in-person interviews with experts on virtually all the early-phase ecosystem players, including investors, founders, accelerators, and others. It took $500,000 and years to complete this study. Fortunately, I was supported by the work of my team, who studied data, articles, and other media sources. This research showed that about 50 percent of startups failed within two years of launch, and nine out of ten failed over the following five years, with investors losing every cent and founders being left out in the cold.

That's a *90 percent* overall failure rate for founders and their startups in the first five years. Another way of looking at it is that just one out of every ten venture-backed startups delivers the projected growth used to justify their original investments. That may be an acceptable—and even profitable—ratio for many portfolio investors, but it's a trap for the vast majority of founders, and I find it heartbreaking. That is the problem with Silicon Valley thinking . . . it's all about the investors, not the founders.

Building a Successful Startup Is Systematic, Yet Unpredictable

After working on my study, I decided to dedicate my life to narrowing the gap between founders who become unicorns and those who risk everything, only to face failure. Teaching people how to become successful builders of startups not only allows people to bring new innovations to life, which drives the evolution of our society, but it also creates economic expansion.

It's personal to me, not only because of the challenges I experienced growing up, but also because, like any first-time founder, I made plenty of avoidable mistakes along the way and came perilously close to hitting bottom. Affiliate Traction, my marketing technology–enabled service, gained some momentum early on, signing up giants like Skechers and American Apparel as our tentpole customers. But along the way, I failed to appreciate the power of the startup lifecycle and underestimated the time it would take to profitability. As a result, like so many others, I took on too much risk.

When the market crashed in 2008, my startup nearly collapsed. In one of the hardest moments of my life, I had to lay off sixty-five employees. Watching their faces and knowing what this meant to their families was a painful experience that I will never forget. Then, I had to look into my wife's eyes and tell her we had to move into a moldy old studio apartment with our two-year-old, relocate the startup headquarters into a barn, and rally a handful of my remaining employees to rebuild the company from the ground up.

With no money coming into the startup, I was only able to pay my bills by going to garage sales, buying beat-up antiques, restoring them, and reselling them at the local market at 5 AM. I was back to scrounging for money just like I had done in my rattlesnake days. This is why I want founders to know how to build a startup carefully and cautiously with a defined plan from start to exit. It is why I don't want them to fall prey to venture capitalists that will leave them with nothing.

While in the process of rebuilding Affiliate Traction, I became a student of the endless list of business operating systems, including Six Sigma, 4DX, Agile, Lean, OGSM, OKRs, and everything else I could find. I tested, tweaked, and applied them to Affiliate Traction. Things eventually got better—*much* better. We signed new customers, including some household names and major brands, like Guess. We hired new employees and brought back some of the old crew. Eventually, in 2016, seventeen years after we'd launched, Affiliate Traction was acquired by eBay Enterprise Marketing Solutions in the deal I mentioned earlier. But I *also* knew that, with a bit more guidance and greater knowledge of what was required to succeed, I could have made it much faster and with fewer white-knuckle moments along the way.

As for the Silicon Valley paradigm (invest in many and see who survives), like plenty of large corporations, it only benefits a small few. But as founders, we can design our own success.

CHAPTER WRAP-UP

While there are many stories about successful Silicon Valley companies, little is written about the many that fail. The point is that you need to be careful before letting investors and others get too deeply involved in your business. You need investment dollars, but you cannot afford to let someone take control of your business.

I would love to hear your thoughts on the book, chapter, or even a section. Simply scan the QR code at the end of every chapter at any time to let me know what you think. I am genuinely interested in your thoughts!

CHAPTER THREE

Where, When, Why, and How Startups Fail (or "The Trouble with Startups")

If you want your startup to succeed, you need to understand why startups fail.

–Tom Eisenmann, Professor of Startup
Administration at Harvard Startup School
and the faculty cochair of the
Arthur Rock Center for Entrepreneurship

This chapter is based on peer-reviewed studies, articles, case studies, government records, academic studies, and the 1,200 one-to-one interviews I mentioned earlier. It also comes from experiencing failures firsthand. One of the most critical insights from all this research was that founders often fail in radically different ways than what you read about in published papers. The reasons published in the trade journals and news articles, that founders *believe* killed their startups, are not necessarily the culprits. This is partly due to how data is collected for these journals and articles, through prepared questionnaires and top-of-mind recollections from founders, which includes any personal biases they may have.

Startup Failure Defined

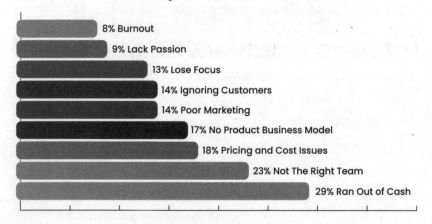

8% Burnout
9% Lack Passion
13% Lose Focus
14% Ignoring Customers
14% Poor Marketing
17% No Product Business Model
18% Pricing and Cost Issues
23% Not The Right Team
29% Ran Out of Cash

Within the 1,200 one-to-one interviews I conducted with founders and investors, among others, I was able to uncover the distinct ways that startups fail, as well as the root cause of the failure. Let's dig into them one by one.

Reason 1–Building the Wrong Management Team

Building a startup is a people game. No matter how good your concept, core technology, or product, your startup will fail unless it has the right team in place. When CB Insights conducted postmortems on over three hundred failed startups,[1] they found seven of the top twenty reasons for startup failures related to people issues and startup culture. Along the same lines, businesses found that 23 percent of tanked startups attributed their losses to problems with their team. In other words, 35 percent of failures were largely due to the people involved in the startup.

There are many *other* triggers for failure—up to and including simply running out of cash—which can be traced back to underlying problems with the people making the decisions. This includes the decision to hire more people than necessary or simply overpay new employees. According to SmartAsset, startups pay an average of over $300,000 in payroll for their first employees. Unfortunately, paying top dollar is no guarantee that your early employees will be able to deliver the results you need.

Of course, every startup founder understands the importance of building a good team. The people you hire early on will shape your culture and your capabilities in critical areas, such as Sales and Marketing, Product and Engineering, Service and Support, and Shared Services, like HR and Finance. But it's important to realize that failure is often baked in, even before you start making your first hires, with the makeup of the founding team itself.

Thousands of horror stories highlight the need for founders to take a long look in the mirror when starting. It's essential not only to be humble but to recognize the things you do well—and even more important, to acknowledge the things you don't do well. As is often stated, it's important to know what you don't know. Perhaps you're a great pitchman for your product but don't have a head for finance, or maybe you're a tech specialist who freezes up like Mark Zuckerberg when the cameras are turned on. Either way, finding the right cofounders and hiring the right startup team can help fill in the gaps in your skill set—as long as you make corrections,

---

1. Emily Hunt, "473 Startup Failure Post-mortems," CB Insights Research, December 16, 2023, https://www.cbinsights.com/research/Startup-failure-post-mortem/.

delegate, and defer when necessary, and have the strength and humility to recognize your own shortcomings.

Another common problem is that founding teams are full of ideas but often unable to build a core product. Looking back on their experience, the founders of recruiting portal Standout Jobs admitted that they'd struggled to create an ideal acquirer profile on their own. They acknowledged that it was a mistake and wrote: "If the founding team can't create a minimum viable product (MVP) on its own (or with a small amount of external help), they shouldn't be founding a startup."[2] I will address this problem later.

Such failures can stem from a lack of technical savvy, but they can equally spring from a lack of alignment among founders about their motivations. You and your team should have the same motivation. To truly be united on the long journey of creating a startup, you need not just to be on the same page, but in the same sentence.

Startups are powered by passion, and building a startup requires an immense amount of self-belief without any self-centeredness. There is no place for the traditional "ego" in startups. Remember, to stay focused, you must be humble! If you aren't all on the same page from the get-go, you're doomed. Alignment is the key. I cannot stress this point enough. Everyone on your team, including you, your leaders, investors, internal staff, and the whole outside team, must see your startup's North Star as clearly as you would on a beautiful summer night. The North Star is your compass. It will ensure you and your team are directionally guided to your end goal. I always tell founders, "If you are crossing the ocean and you are one degree off, you will end up on the wrong continent." What often happens with startups is that they lose their way, but if they have a North Star, they can always orient themselves to that one guiding star. At one

---

2. Ben Yoskovitz, "Instigator Blog," October 5, 2010, https://www.instigatorblog.com /postmortem-analysis-of-standout-jobs/2010/10/05/.

time, because of its consistent location in the sky, sailors literally used the North Star as a navigation tool.

Without an alignment of purpose, goals, and direction, it is easy for founders and their teams to lose interest, become disconnected, and get pulled in different directions. This leads to arguments rather than team creativity. Later, I will talk more about the North Star, which is designed to solve this problem.

The most successful startups are intrinsically motivated teams. They are personally deriving satisfaction from seeing it come to fruition. Assembling a group of people who are motivated primarily by the thought of accumulating wealth, or what I call "coin-operated," is very dangerous. You will lose them and their interest in the project easily, because money creates an appetite, and building a startup requires much more than the desire for wealth.

Finally, a word of caution: hiring the right people doesn't always mean hiring *more* people. At the start, you need grit, grind, and people that have an "I'll do it" mentality, not an "I'll need to hire someone for that job" or "that's not my job" mentality. At one startup in which I recently made an investment, the founding team was made up of former executives and consultants, and all they knew was how to hire *practitioners to do the work*. The CEO couldn't wrap his head around the notion that his tiny startup didn't need a phalanx of C-level managers. Ultimately, he had to step aside so we could build the right-sized team, capable of delivering the required results. It was a messy situation and one that could have been avoided with a clearer understanding of the purpose by the founding team.

Reason 2–Targeting the Wrong Customers

It might sound counterintuitive, but the thousands of one-to-one interviews taught me that startups also fail because founders target the wrong customers. In fact, according to CB Insights' postmortems, nine of the top twenty reasons for startup failures—and five out of the top ten—are related to failure to engage customers effectively.[3] As I write this, I recall a startup of mine that targeted customers who we later came to find out were not "technology natives" and had an old-school "let's meet in person" profile. This persona made it so that our traditional content marketing did not work.

One of the first questions that startups need to answer is: Who will buy their products? I sometimes wonder how so many startups get this simple question so badly wrong.

The key is to recognize up front the value you will offer customers, without which you have no business. If you aren't creating value for customers, it doesn't matter what your logo looks like or what your startup offers employees in a benefits package.

As an investor, if I walk into a prime office space with a startup asking for funding, I first ask how much this office space costs. I have had startups give me "swag" gifts and show me the new beanbag chairs for their conference room. These are all things that founders do to make their startup look better in the beginning. I say, rather than sprucing up the office, be frugal and stay relentlessly focused on your customers' pain points, and you'll be far more likely to build a product that has real value in the marketplace. At that point, everything else will follow, including investors.

Understand your customer like you understand your family, best friends, and children. That is to say, you have to understand, as much as possible, who they are, where they go, what they like to have/buy, what matters to them, and how they think. We'll explore your *ideal customer profiles* and *personas* in detail later.

---

3. Emily Hunt, "473 Startup Failure Post-mortems," CB Insights Research, December 16, 2023, https://www.cbinsights.com/research/Startup-failure-post-mortem/.

Remember, the "right" customer isn't *just* one who'll happily buy your product. The goal isn't to sell a widget today—it's to build a startup that you can sell tomorrow. That means building a regular/steady customer base that can serve as stepping stones to more customers and market sectors. To grow and build value, you'll need to be able to strategically expand from your initial beachhead out into a broader cross section of the marketplace. Many strategies—such as "Land and Expand," whereby you get your foot in the door by entering the marketplace with a small product and then build/expand from there to more products, or the Lobster Trap approach, where you offer something so attractive that customers just walk in to get to it, like a lobster crawling in to get the food, but can't easily walk away—may be successful in the short term but detrimental to the continued growth of your startup in the long term. Think past short-term gains and focus on the customers' outcome. Success does not come from what you do occasionally; it comes from what you do consistently.

Find customers aligned, not just with your offerings, but also with whoever will hopefully acquire your startup in the future. Remember, where you are next year depends on what you do now. For example, if your long-term plan is to be acquired by Salesforce, you must ensure that their customer and your customer are the same. Virtually all acquisitions are strategic synergies to benefit the acquirer by saving or making money, expanding features, getting more "share of wallet," or nefariously burying the competition, with the ultimate goal of consistent profitable growth to move stock prices.

You won't have the exit (sale) you are looking for if your customer does not match your desired acquirer's ideal customer profile and persona. This customer qualification must happen as early as possible. Therefore, from day one, you need to know what characterizes the ideal customer, not solely for your product(s), but for your business . . . which leads to the number three reason startups (built to sell) fail.

Reason 3—Overlooking the Exit Strategy from the Start

I recently got my hands on an off-road electric skateboard. It's amazing. It's capable of hurtling adults uphill at 25 mph or more. When you're on it, you feel like you're flying. Until you hit a rock on the trail and a wheel comes off, and suddenly, you *are* flying—right into the ground. In the split second between leaving and hitting the ground, my only thought was, *Oh shit. This is really going to hurt!*

Later, during my long stay in the hospital, I had time to reflect on the importance of having a clear plan for *what happens next* and *thinking ahead.* Building a startup is like a skateboard going faster than your ability to control it and taking the chance that the wheels will stay attached while traveling at high speeds when you hit a rock. That's a terrible idea if you're a middle-aged dude riding a toy designed for teenagers. But it's potentially an even greater risk if you're building a startup and have your investors' money, your future, and the livelihoods of your employees in your hands, riding that skateboard with you.

Incredibly, 95 percent of founders start with little or no idea of their exit strategy. Of course, a portion of this 95 percent may be building lifestyle businesses that they may or may not sell someday or that may be turned over to their offspring. Remember, you are building a startup designed to sell so your investors receive a significant return and become wealth independent, while solving a worthwhile problem.

As an investor, I review around one hundred deals every month, and I am always amazed that very few have any idea of their exit strategy. Investors tell me, "It's too early," and founders usually say something like, "Well, we think it could be . . ." Why is this so important to know as a founder looking for a successful exit? Because understanding what type of startups your potential acquirers are buying, at what price, and under what terms is a critical part of your overall strategy.

When considering who you will sell your startup to, reflect on these three questions:

1. Do I know how many startups my potential acquirer(s) have previously acquired?
2. What were the terms of those transactions?
3. Do their customers match my customers?

Remember, there may be one hundred startups for five well-researched potential target acquirers, so it's like musical chairs, where someone will constantly be left standing. These things are critical to helping you avoid the problem of not understanding your exit strategy from day one. Hopes and dreams are motivating when you're whizzing along in the early days, but all too soon, reality comes calling, and like me on the skateboard, you may come crashing down and hit the ground hard.

The bottom line is that acquirers buy startups to save or make money. Therefore, the startup you are trying to exit must either save or make the acquirer money, and you can't make money without a solid product. For example, in the case of making more money, acquirers buy startups to add new products to sell to their existing customers, thereby growing their customers' lifetime value. By growing the lifetime value, you increase your overall revenue per customer, thus increasing the lifetime value to customer acquisition cost ratio, which is a key driver. Now, imagine if you do not know who your potential acquirer has as a customer. You may spend huge amounts of money on your go-to-market strategy, getting customers your acquirer does not want, and thus has no interest in acquiring. It's simple math. No deal.

Acquisitions are about outcomes, and outcomes are best preplanned. Here is another way to think about it. If your whole startup is a product to be sold to an acquirer, why would you build a startup without knowing who wants to acquire it? That's essentially the same as creating a product without a customer in mind!

I have had many arguments with founders and investors when I advise them to start planning their exit at the beginning of their journey rather than waiting until later. If I had a nickel for every time I heard "It's too early . . ." After explaining my rationale, founders and investors almost always agree with me. If you want to build a business with the goal of selling it to a large behemoth of a company, you need to plan your exit from the start. Be the company your acquirers want!

Reason 4–Overvaluing Your Startup

Overvaluation isn't just a problem for startups like WeWork, which drew investments by promising outlandish returns, even while racking up multibillion-dollar losses.[4,5] It has been an ongoing concern of investors and potential acquirers for a number of years. For example, Getaround, a car-sharing marketplace, went public after a merger with InterPrivate II Acquisition Corp, in December of 2022. They set an initial valuation for the company of $1.2 billion. Shares have dropped significantly since. In fact, 2022 brought the largest drop in valuations in history, with companies like Instacart dropping 15 percent.

What does this mean? It means, while high valuations still exist, caution is strongly advised. Those of us who struggled through the dot-com bomb in 2000 remember how overvaluation can cause nightmarish results. Among the companies at that time that rode the wave of overvaluations was Nortel, the Canadian telecommunications company that saw the company's share price increase tenfold from the start of 1997 until it peaked in September 2000, largely from the purchase of (often

---

4. Nicole Gelinas for CNN Business Perspectives, "WeWork's Downfall Shows How Ridiculously Overvalued So Many Startups Are," CNN, September 26, 2019, https://www.cnn.com/2019/09/26/perspectives/wework-Startups-overvalued/index.html.

5. Roger L. Martin, "The Overvaluation Trap," Harvard Business Review, n.d., https://hbr.org/2015/12/the-overvaluation-trap.

overvalued) smaller tech startups that were bought with overpriced Nortel stock. In 2000, Nortel's market cap peaked at $283 billion. Then everything turned upside down, and within the next two years, Nortel's market dropped to less than $5 billion. Nonetheless, high valuations didn't stop Adobe's $20 billion Figma acquisition, proving that high valuations are still out there, even in a down market for investors.

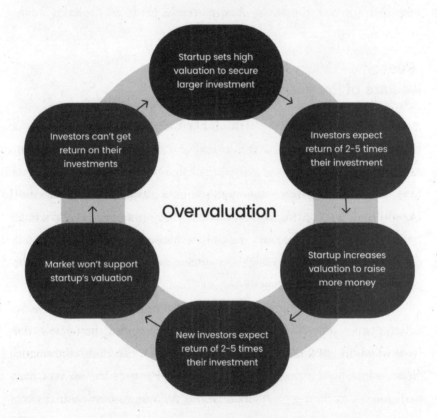

False inflation often happens when startup founders without a capital strategy (aka a plan that looks into the future) look only at their closest comparable valuation. You may recognize the word "comparables" from buying your first home, having an appraisal done and comparing it to the "high/low" homes in your neighborhood. You would then use this information to help decide on the home price you'd offer. This is just a start to understanding the huge gray cloud surrounding valuations. If you know that startups like yours sell for $50M, you need to consider not valuing yourself past that figure, and if you do, you had better have a *really* good reason. Remember what I said about musical chairs? Investors, however, are looking for five to ten times that number in return. Therefore, if you raise $500K at a $1M pre-money value, your value is $1.5M. But, and this is a *big* but, your investors are thinking $7.5M to keep their interest. Promising outsized results to attract capital is a dangerous misstep.

Beware of Promising Unicorn Status

A startup aiming for unicorn status is like a teenager telling their parents that they want to be a rock star. The reality is that, based on my research, less than 0.0010 percent of startups achieve unicorn status, so if your plans are to have any real value, then you need more realistic goals. Aiming too high and getting your valuation wrong puts you on the wrong trajectory from the get-go and guarantees that, eventually, you'll run out of runway. Too often, a sky-high valuation leads to what Eric Ries, author of *The Lean Startup*, memorably terms "success theater," with founders putting time and energy into projecting success that would have been better spent on improving their products or better serving their customers. In other words, startups that are valued too high for their current startup phase feel the need to demonstrate their value by *performing* success rather than staying focused on actually *achieving* success. And, of course, once you give in to the temptation to overvalue yourself, it's hard to take a step back off the carousel. Your early investors won't let you walk back your past promises, so you'll find yourself seeking to project more and more success and inflating your value further and further to keep your backers happy. Such a higher valuation also means you've received more money, potentially hiring more people than you need, building up a burn rate you simply can't sustain, and locking yourself into a path that can only be sustained with constant injections of additional capital. When your investors catch on, they'll put away their checkbooks, and your startup won't be long for this world.

To avoid these problems, many of the smartest startup founders stay nimble and lean early, making every dollar count while growing their startups. Instagram, for instance, took just $500K in seed money while it was building its product and demonstrating its staying power, and Tumblr took $750K in series A funding. Both startups ultimately achieved $1B+ exits *because* of (not in *spite* of) their restrained approach early on. Remember, the goal of acquirers is to make money or save money, so the costlier it is to run the business you are selling, the harder it gets for them to reach their goal.

One final word of caution: I often speak to founders who think that getting a high valuation early on is the best way to reduce dilution, which is a reduction in the value of ownership for each shareholder in the startup. The reality, though, is that dilution is a process that needs to be managed over a period of years, based on the way your startup is legally structured, not one that you can deal with (or prevent) simply by jacking up your valuation at the outset. Building a startup is a marathon, not a sprint, so there is time to increase the real value and offset the dilution. To achieve life-changing wealth for yourself and your cofounders, it pays to keep your dreams and ambitions in check early on and maintain as much ownership as possible by controlling valuation and investment amounts.

I always encourage founders to explore and use non-dilutive funding options, such as grants, loans, or anything from which you are getting money without giving away equity, which you can find in the Visionaries platform (at the QR code at the end of this chapter). This is especially important early on, when valuations can be low. Before taking seed money, exhaust your potential non-dilutive forms of capital.

Reason 5—Listening to Bad Advice

In the beginning of a startup journey, it's best to pay close attention to all the good advice you receive and to completely ignore all the bad advice you receive. Of course, the trick lies in figuring out which is which. In the beginning, *everyone* has an opinion. But not everyone has an opinion that's worth listening to. Some people have their own agendas. I have found that, in some cases, consultants and mentors who offer free advice are actually offering free advice trying to drum up business. Other advisors may be looking for paid board seats, while accountants, lawyers, and vendors may be looking for new customers and investors but have never actually built a startup. Among my personal favorites are the one-hit wonders who suddenly think they are experts. It's like a rookie hitting a home run and then assuming he could now be a hitting coach.

Then there is the all-too-common program manager who regurgitates what they have seen, studied, and heard, but who has never actually experienced it themselves, and certainly has not had to pay the consequences when things went wrong. Advice, if you act on it, should be something you interview for. Like the saying goes, "Beware the naked man who offers you his shirt."

It's one thing to read about or watch other people ski down a mountain, but it's a whole other thing to do it yourself. Even your investors' interests aren't necessarily aligned with your own, which means their advice may be linked to their own agendas. Angel investors, venture capitalists (VCs), and bankers certainly want to see you succeed—but they want to see you make it *big at all costs*. They want you to deliver outsized returns that can offset their bets on other startups that fail altogether. That means the optimal risk level for an investor betting on multiple startups is typically quite a bit higher than the optimal level for a founder, who has one shot at building a successful startup.

As we noted in the chapter on Silicon Valley, VCs bet on many startups, so your startup failure would be just one more write-off for them. For you, it could prove devastating. It's also worth remembering that, generally, investors aren't practitioners, and many don't have the background and experience of being a founder. That means they typically lack operational experience. An investor might have strong opinions about how to build a successful startup, but they have usually spent most of their career as a passenger, not a driver.

In short . . . before you take (or act on) anyone's advice, get at least a second opinion.

So, Who Can You Listen To?

Well, I might be biased, but I'd say you should chiefly seek advice from founders who've proven their chops by steering at least two, preferably three or more, startups to successful exits.

The key is to engage and to ensure you filter out the genuinely applicable and useful advice from the rest of the noise. It's always tempting to go with your gut instinct, which is a 50-50 shot at best. It's also important to remember confirmation bias and judge the value of the advice you receive from a logical perspective, not an emotional one. You'll want to pay close attention to the background, experience, and possible agenda of anyone who gives you counsel.

Beyond that, there are two main places to get insights. One is from people who've tried and failed to build a startup—because knowing what *not* to do is always important. A failed founder might not be able to tell you in which direction to head, but they can certainly tell you where not to go, and why, by explaining the consequences of their decisions.

The other place to seek advice is from domain-specific experts. If you're dealing with a legal question, by all means ask a lawyer with experience in cases like yours. And if you're looking for help overcoming a technical issue, call in a specialist who knows about the specific tech challenge you're trying to solve. If you're like me and want to write a book, get a writer. Don't assume that your lawyer, accountant, or favorite software guru is *also* an expert at running a successful startup.

Also, look for vertical subject matter experts or functional subject matter experts. For example, when I first trained for a marathon, I quite naturally sought advice from marathon runners. But I soon found that people who'd run just a single marathon and people who'd run ten or more races had quite different things to say—and the more experienced runners had more useful advice for me, because they'd had time to notice patterns and derive knowledge from a deep understanding of the process of running a race. Simple things like shoes, socks, water, and snacks can massively change a runner's outcome. Seek out people with beat-up, well-worn sneakers, instead of near-pristine, barely broken-in running shoes, and you'll generally get better advice. Don't be scared. There is an old French proverb that says, "To believe a thing impossible is to make it so."

You may end up taking some bad advice—we've all done that. It's part of failing, which is part and parcel of having success. The only way not to fail, whether it's through bad advice or trying something you believed would work but did not, is simply by not trying at all. Every success story is littered with small failures along the way. Those failures are a standard part of every startup's lifecycle. Like my mom used to say, "Failure is another word for progress." Nonetheless, you want to keep failures small, manageable, and actionable—and you want to take note of your failures so you can learn from them. As Einstein said about making a mistake, "One time is an accident. Doing it twice is a decision." Also, keep in mind that recognizing small failures helps you avoid larger ones.

And finally, consider the words of NBA legend Michael Jordan, who was quoted as saying during his playing days: "I've missed more than nine thousand shots in my career. I've lost over three hundred games. Twenty-six times I've been trusted to take the game winning shot and missed. I've failed over and over and over again in my life. And that is why I succeed."

CHAPTER WRAP-UP

In this chapter, I've given you a sense of where big failures often occur for new startups. You might want to keep a list of the five reasons for failure mentioned in this chapter nearby so you will remember them as you proceed. As you move through the book, I will point out failures in the context of the Startup Science Lifecycle, in line with the chapters, so you don't make the same mistakes.

The Seven-Phase Startup Science Lifecycle

The Seven Phases: An Introduction

In the upcoming chapters, I will provide a detailed overview of each phase your startup will pass through on the way to a successful exit. As you proceed, you will notice that the phases will build on each other as your startup matures. There is a lot to think about during each phase, and plenty of research necessary, so staying organized and following the process carefully will make it easier to move through the phases.

Key Performance Indicators

You will see as you read through the seven phases of a startup that there will be an increasing focus on key performance indicators (KPIs). They will be an integral part of your journey, especially as you head through the later chapters, where you will need to measure your progress carefully prior to preparing for an exit.

Let me give you a little "real-world" example of KPIs in action. As I write this book, I am training for a marathon swim, and I hate it when my Apple Watch tracks my swim, and then stubbornly refuses to applaud me for achieving my daily target. But I also know that the only way to achieve my goal is to put the work in. Without visibility into how much I am actually swimming, it's easy to cut corners, make excuses, and procrastinate, but thanks to my Apple Watch, I have KPIs with which I cannot argue, or ignore. Just as my Apple Watch counts steps, startups need "in your face data" that can be acted upon all throughout the startup process.

Regarding measurements and metrics, Peter Drucker, the inventor of the concept "managing by objective," famously said, "What gets measured gets done."

Remember, you will definitely have challenges as you proceed. Don't panic. Challenges are part of the startup process for all of us. Below is a brief introductory overview of the phases you will be reading about.

Phase One: VISION (and Finding Your North Star)

The Startup Science Lifecycle journey starts in the Vision phase, which includes defining your ecosystem, performing product ideation, setting your strategic vision, and building your North Star so you can see exactly where you want to be, which is like putting your final destination into a GPS. Your North Star helps you avoid roadblocks and plots the most efficient path to achieving your objectives. You'll use your North Star to validate your vision and product ideation with advisors, including industry experts and potential future customers.

- Failure Risk: Level 1: Frequent (likely to occur, to be expected)
- Round: Pre-seed

- Cycle-Time: 3–6 months
- Average Round: $100K to $500K
- Benchmark Phase Failure Rate: 50 percent
- Average Valuation: $250K to $1M

Phase Two: PRODUCT

With a validated North Star, your startup will move on to the Product phase, where you'll produce and—with the help of your advisory board—validate a prototype and minimum viable product. You will also structure and test your basic go-to-market strategies. This is the point where you'll likely begin hiring employees and building your functional areas.

- Failure Risk: Level 2: Probable (likely to occur, not surprised)
- Round: Seed
- Cycle-Time: Months 12 to 24
- Average Round: $1M to $5M
- Failure Rate: 30 percent
- Average Valuation: $500K to $2M

Phase Three: GO-TO-MARKET

With a validated product, you'll be ready to proceed to the Go-to-Market phase, where you'll execute, assess, and refine your go-to-market strategies at a small scale. Your objective is to demonstrate to investors that your company has the potential to be cash-flow positive—you have a product customers will buy and effective marketing strategies to capture their attention.

- Failure Risk: Level 3: Elevated (Less likely to occur, not surprised)
- Round: Series seed
- Cycle-Time: Months 24 to 36
- Average Round: $2M to $10M

- Failure Rate: 25 percent
- Average Valuation: $2M to $5M

Phase Four: STANDARDIZATION

In the Standardization phase, you'll document the best practices you will use to achieve success and then deploy them throughout your company. Standardization reduces risk and increases investor confidence, essential steps as you seek more capital to grow.

- Failure Risk: Level 4: Moderate (unlikely to occur, surprised)
- Round: A Round
- Cycle-Time: Months 24 to 48
- Average Round: $5M to $50M
- Failure Rate: 20 percent
- Average Valuation: $5M to $10M (you can expect this range to change frequently, since it's subject to market conditions)

Phase Five: OPTIMIZATION

Once you've standardized your operations across the board, you'll enter the Optimization phase. While continuing to execute and improve best practices, you'll use KPIs to find opportunities to reduce waste and increase profit margin. Optimization primes your company for scalable growth.

- Failure Risk: Level 5: Occasional (likely to occur occasionally)
- Round: B Round
- Cycle-Time: Months 24 to 48
- Average Round: $25M to $100M
- Failure Rate: 20 percent
- Average Valuation: 15 to 20 percent higher than A Round

Phase Six: GROWTH

During the Growth phase, you'll align your entire company toward the KPIs, which increases margin, which your potential acquirers value most. You'll apply investor capital toward scaling your customer base with your efficient, well-documented operations, maximizing your company's value as you prepare for exit.

- Failure Risk: Level 6: Remote (unlikely, though possible)
- Round: C Round
- Cycle-Time: Months 24 to 60
- Average Round: $25M to $100M
- Failure Rate: 20 percent
- Average Valuation: 15 to 20 percent higher than B Round

Phase Seven: EXIT

Finally, you'll enter the Exit phase, where you'll foster relationships and partnerships with potential acquirers as they perform due diligence assessments of your optimized machine. After many years of hard work, you'll negotiate a profitable exit that meets investor targets and makes you wealthy.

- Failure Risk: Level 6: Remote (unlikely, though possible)
- Round: D Round
- Cycle-Time: Months 24 to 60
- Average Round: $25M to $100M
- Failure Rate: 20 percent
- Average Valuation: 15 to 20 percent higher than C Round

As you can see, the seven phases provide a fluid plan for creating, nurturing, growing, and selling your startup. Let me illustrate, briefly, the benefit of having such a plan in place.

One summer, I spent months building my truck for an epic three-month off-road on-road overland trip with my family. We hit thirteen national parks and some crazy off-road trails and, at times, were completely alone out in the wild. The truck was fitted with water storage, power storage, solar, and sleeping for four. I had planned where we were going, when we would arrive, and how long it would take, so I knew what we needed regarding fuel, food, and water. I had a map that provided the route, and I knew where the trail would get difficult, with obstacles I would need to navigate slowly around and which would require my strict attention. Like all trips, unexpected things happened, but I had done this before, so I prepared for the unexpected.

On this trip, as always, I was thinking about the founder's experience. Founders that have done none of this preparation, but talk about an epic trip, wonder why they fail. They are walking around in the darkness with a flashlight, and the only thing they see is what the light hits. As a result, they stumble, trip, and fall, get up again, and walk into a wall. Founders focus on funding, because that's all they can see, the mighty dollar. They need someone to turn on the lights to see the whole room. When I talk to founders, they constantly tell me, "I need funding." So, I explain the same thing every time: funding, like wealth, is an outcome, not a plan.

Like many parents, when my first baby was born, I started thinking, this baby could not survive without us. As she began to grow and became an adult, I realized I was less a parent and more a mentor. Startups are very much the same. They start as infants, move through childhood, become teenagers, and finally move out independently. The Startup Science Lifecycle is analogous to these phases of development. '

The lifecycle graphic below shows the entire trajectory of a successful startup. This chart routinely makes people lean back, tilt their heads, and say, "*Ohhhh*. Now I get it!"

The Startup Science Lifecycle is a compilation of hard-won insights that many startup veterans have arrived at, almost intuitively, over their

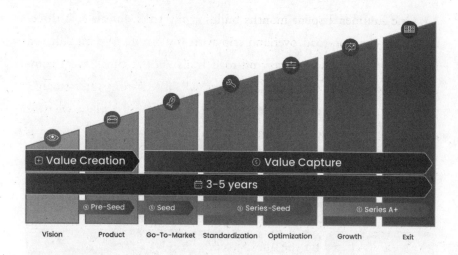

years in the industry. Besides illustrating the trajectory of a startup, a secondary benefit is that it standardizes the language that founders and investors use to discuss their startups and what will be most helpful in ensuring continued success. Every conversation I have with a founder starts with identifying which phase they are currently in, and understanding the missions or steps they need to satisfy in order to continue their progress.

In the following chapters, we will explore each phase in greater detail. As you will see, the phases fall into two key processes:

First there is value creation, which includes having an idea for a product or service that solves a problem and then building a product prototype and getting feedback and validation of your idea.

VALUE CREATION PHASES:

- VISION
- PRODUCT

Then there are the value capture phases, which focus on taking your product(s) to market, making the necessary alterations, while growing your business to the point where you will have a successful exit.

VALUE CAPTURE PHASES:

- GO-TO-MARKET
- STANDARDIZATION
- OPTIMIZATION
- GROWTH
- EXIT

Understanding where your startup is relative to the lifecycle is important, because it provides a standardized framework to help you clearly comprehend the missions that need to be accomplished, objectives that need to be completed, tasks needed to accomplish those objectives, and the metrics that track progress and performance.

Moving through each phase requires a series of necessary steps as you prepare to engage with investors and/or move smoothly through the lifecycle. Learning to take these steps in sequential order, and at the right time, ensures that what you work on is phase-appropriate and that you've done the foundational work required to progress to the next phase with foresight and intention.

Identifying Where You Are on the Lifecycle

The Startup Science Lifecycle makes understanding the process of running a startup sound pretty simple. That's by design because, in some ways, it *is* simple: putting one foot in front of the other, in the right order.

In practice, things are a bit more complicated than that. As a startup founder, you're constantly struggling against the fog and friction of battle, and it can be hard to understand exactly what your current weaknesses are or what needs doing next. If you want to go from one place to another, you must know two things to start: first, you need to know where you are, and second, you need to know where you are going. One of the hardest things to figure out is *where* on the Startup Science Lifecycle you currently stand—and if you don't know where you are, you're guaranteed to get lost.

I learned this logic when I backpacked the 220 miles of the John Muir Trail. I'd arranged for necessary supplies to be brought in on pack mules, but I had a one-day window to meet the supply team before they would need to move on. I was running late, so I hiked through the night to make up lost time—and that's when I had the bright idea of trying to take a shortcut.

Well, it went about as well as you'd expect. Sometime around 1 AM, I found myself stumbling through a snowfield, with no idea where I was, and "snow blind" by the glare of the moonlight on the whiteness all around me. It took me longer than it should have, and I must admit I was utterly lost. Eventually, I got down on my knees to feel my footprints, which were frozen into the snow behind me, and followed them back down the mountainside until I hit a riverbank. From there, I could trace my way back to the trail and, eventually—chastened, exhausted, and half-hypothermic—I was able to make my way to the resupply site the next morning, just in time to grab my supplies.

I managed to get my bearings back and pushed through the rest of the 220 miles and thirty mountains of the John Muir Trail. Founders can get "snow blind" by the sheer number of tasks and objectives, but remember the importance of having a real plan. Don't simply stride off into the wilderness.

Know Where You Are Going

Like the mountaineering analogy above, you can't afford to get lost when you have limited supplies, energy, and resources. This is something I see all the time as I meet with founders. Often, a founder will sit down for a meeting, thinking they're ready for a round of funding—only for it to become apparent, after a bit of digging, that they have not yet ticked the crucial boxes you'd expect a startup to take care of during the pre-seed or seed phases.

Such crucial boxes include a number of important documents. These are pretty standard and include:

- References and corporate documents, such as anything related to the legal and organizational structure of your company
- Business plans and financials
- Market research data
- Intellectual properties that you have or have applied for, such as patents, trademarks, copyrights, and domain names
- Shareholder information and agreements
- Material agreements
- Documents pertaining to risks or potential litigation
- Employee relations and benefits
- Equity grants

When I ask founders what they will use the funds for, the first answer is always vague, so I dig down, using the five whys, based on Toyota's Five Principles, which are part of the Toyota Production System.

Getting founders to understand that they've left important work undone isn't always easy. (Sometimes, if it's a startup I care strongly about, there's some heated conversation involved.) Fortunately, it's usually possible to course correct as necessary in such cases. But getting things right the first time is much easier and more efficient, which means tracking your progress through the lifecycle, to ensure you aren't missing steps or getting ahead of yourself.

CHAPTER WRAP-UP

In this chapter we introduced the seven phases of a startup and emphasized the significance of KPIs and driving value throughout the phases ahead. It's important to recognize which phase you are in and know when it is time to move sequentially to the next phase. There is no set time limit for the phases. Some, like Phase One, will encompass more planning and research, while other phases may move more quickly.

Now on to the main event: the seven phases of the Startup Science Lifecycle.

Phase One (Part 1): Vision and North Star

> You read a book from beginning to end. You run a
> startup the opposite way. You start with the end, and
> then you do everything you must to reach it.
> **–Harold S. Geneen, who grew ITT from $765 million
> in sales in 1961 to $17 billion in sales in 1970,
> with more than 350 acquisitions and mergers
> in eighty countries**

The science of manifesting a vision into a successful startup begins not with a founder's epiphany, but rather in methodically validating your idea and proving it beyond any doubt—to yourself, potential investors, future customers, and possible acquirers. It's important not to get dazzled by that initial flash of brilliant creativity that sparks your startup vision. Always remember, the initial idea is an art. Building the startup is the science.

The plain truth is that even the best vision is doomed to fall short unless it is accompanied by the important, albeit often lengthy, process of creating your North Star. This is what you will learn in this chapter.

Vision

Remember, your vision is why you are starting your business in the first place. It will align with your business goals and aspirations. One of the easiest ways I can connect you to why vision is so important is by telling you my El Capitan story. When I was in my twenties, I had the idea to climb El Capitan, a three-thousand-foot vertical rock formation in Yosemite National Park. I could have put my head down, joined a climbing gym, and convinced myself that that was sufficient enough to conquer one of the most difficult climbing challenges in the world. That would have meant I was self-validating my vision and likely following a recipe for failure.

You can't effectively validate your own vision. If you sit around focusing on your own idea, it's way too easy to do what we call "drink your own lemonade" and succumb to your biases, overlook flaws, and convince yourself that your vision is bulletproof. Instead, you need *external* validation. But, before you can seek external validation for your idea, and secure your first outside investors (and no, your credit card and rich great-uncle don't count), you'll need to clearly show how your vision can be translated into a real and successful startup. This means you can clearly demonstrate that you can turn your vision into a minimum viable product. You do this by defining your North Star.

I found experienced advisors and climbers who validated that it was a realistic idea for an inexperienced climber to train for, and bag, El Capitan. I listened to the experts' guidance on which parts of the climb generally cause people to struggle, how to train for those challenges, and which gear to buy. I stayed in touch with these experts, kept them updated on my progress, and spent time training with many. The result was a challenging, but successful, climb of El Capitan.

The alchemy that sparks a successful startup concept (vision) is one I cannot teach, replicate, or reverse engineer, and it certainly can't be forced. In fact, to anyone who has not experienced it firsthand, the process of dreaming up a new startup looks a bit like black magic.

My hypothesis behind StartupScience.io is based on the conviction that creating a startup can be approached scientifically with a reasonable expectation of success.

North Star

My North Star is to reduce the startup failure rate and evolve the world and everything on it. I do this by helping founders succeed so their products and innovations become reality. My long version is "A broad collaboration focused on the startup ecosystem that places inclusion, environmental, and sustainability as key foundational principles to ensure that Startup Science.io supports a diverse range of stakeholders, including underserved populations. StartupScience.io is also committed to supporting and advancing business solutions that contribute to some of the world's most pressing social and environmental challenges in sectors and thematic areas that include the environment, clean energy, health, food security, water, national security, and the Global Sustainability Goals, to name a few."

Startups change the world, and I truly believe that, if I can help even just a little, by making a dent in the two problems that led me to want to write this book, we can create a better world for all of us and the planet, equally.

In creating your startup, remember that the North Star represents your startup's definition of its purpose, its products, its customers, and potential acquirers. Clarity about a North Star leads founders and start-ups toward their goals and helps investors envision the startup's future growth. Here is where vision and North Star come together.

Without a North Star guiding your startup, the chance of failing is almost 100 percent. A clearly defined North Star leads founders and start-ups toward their goals and helps investors envision the startup's future growth. Of course, I learned this the hard way! The most humiliated I have ever felt was during a pitch meeting in New York City with Goldman Sachs. I was on a road show to raise cash for my biotech startup. The CEO of the business that eventually acquired my business, Bill, a kind, smart, and dear friend to this day, had arranged the meeting.

I still remember going up in the elevators and the doors opening right into an office full of rich wood, finely dressed people, and spectacular views of New York City. I remember feeling very insecure, and so out of my element at the time. I was sent to a conference room, followed shortly by eight people, talking as they entered the room. I sat patiently as they spoke to each other. Then, after a short time, I started into my pitch.

Within five minutes, two of the eight just got up and left without saying a word. Five minutes later, another two left . . . then another two. Eventually, there were only two people besides me remaining in the con-ference room.

I paused, my face red, feeling a combination of embarrassment and humiliation. I felt my childhood. I straightened up and said, "Listen, I realize that the two of you are probably staying here because of Bill, and it's clear that I have made some mistakes, and if I could just use half of the time I have left for feedback, I would greatly appreciate it."

One of the investors, who we'll call Gray Suit, as he was wearing a shiny, perfectly fitted gray suit, said, "How about we do lunch instead?"

I was happy to get out of the situation and agreed. Over lunch, Gray Suit spoke about pitch after pitch, good, bad, and ugly (mine was ugly). He explained what was needed and what could be left behind.

Gray Suit said, "Greg, if an architect promised to build you your dream home, but couldn't show you blueprints and models, or describe the concept in a way that gave you a mental picture, you'd take that as a pretty big red flag, yes?" He went on to explain that investors take the same view of founders who can't explain their vision. While they might know the market, they aren't the right person to turn that vision into a startup.

This experience, and Gray Suit's words, motivated me to create my North Star, a collection of data that not only described my startup in a way that covered the essential basics, but in a way that allowed my vision to be operationalized.

When founders begin building their startups without establishing a North Star, they risk traveling in directions that won't yield the desired outcomes—and, in many cases, they don't realize it until it's too late to correct the course.

In fact, the data, according to CB Insights, shows that:

- 14 percent of small startups fail because they ignore their customers' needs
- 19 percent fail due to competition
- 13 percent fail as a result of disagreements
- 13 percent fail due to a loss of focus

All of the statistics above are due to a lack of alignment and candid research from the start. And since the earth rotates, and the world around you changes, you will need to continually update your North Star, and continue to use it for guidance until the day you sell your startup.

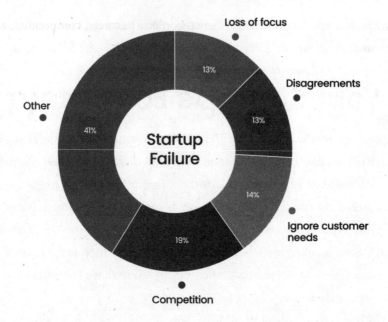

First Round of Investments

Typically, your very first funding round comes from family, friends, and crowdfunding. Startups in Phase One typically raise their first round of external funding, often colloquially known as pre-seed capital, in the region of $50,000 to $500,000, with current startup valuations of somewhere between $250,000 and $2M. You can also look for grants, as well as funding from winning pitch competitions, by scanning the QR code at the end of this chapter.

The Ecosystem

Creating your ecosystem provides you with a tapestry of your startup's universe. It is one of the most important tasks and one of the most useful and important things you can do at this phase (Vision) in your startup, and it should be redone every year. Updating your ecosystem will also lead you to take actions related to customers, partners, competitors, and potential acquirers.

Your Startup's Ecosystem

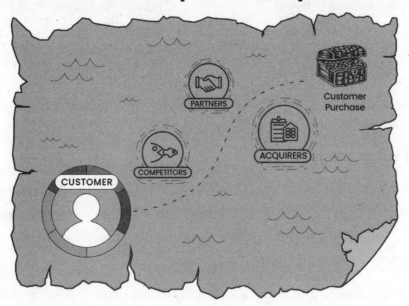

My biotech startup venture focused on marketing and distributing water treatment solutions that use microbes to eliminate hydrocarbons and reduce the production of waste in water. Our main customers were municipalities and commercial fish and shrimp farms that used our technology to eliminate the "gunk" that accumulated in their ponds after each harvest.

Our acquirer was a large, publicly traded Canadian company, in an all-stock deal that left me a paper millionaire. Soon after the acquisition, using our startup's ecosystem, the company acquired a swath of shrimp farms in Central and South America.

This story illustrates how your ecosystem provides a landscape of your entire potential industry and markets; it's your world within the greater world. The goal of your ecosystem document is to help you and your acquirer understand where your product vision would place your startup on the industry landscape.

The BOSS Ecosystem Template					
Company Name	Industry/Vertical	Type	Stage	Website	Social Media
Drones R Us	Commercial Drones	Competitor	Mature	🔗	@dronesplus
Bullseye Drones	Commercial Drones	Acquirer	Mature	🔗	@bullseyedrone
Halo Control Systems	Aerospace Control Systems	Partner	Mature	🔗	@halocontrols

Market Identification and Sizing

Serviceable obtainable market (SOM), serviceable addressable market (SAM), and total addressable market (TAM) are all relative market sizes and revenue amounts that represent paths of growth for your startup.

- Serviceable obtainable market (SOM) is the market share and revenue that you *will* realistically capture and service in the next twelve months, without any investor funding (or additional funding, if you've already received some).
- Serviceable addressable market (SAM) is the market share and revenue that you *could* potentially capture and service in the next twelve months, if you received the investor funding necessary for product development, marketing, and service delivery.
- Total addressable market (TAM) is the number of customers and annual revenue you could generate if your startup theoretically captured 100 percent market share in the future. Investors look at TAM to ensure there's available market share in which your startup can grow. TAM also guides you in thinking about the market you are serving, the extent of your product-market fit, and your growth road map.

When communicating target markets to investors, I start with SOM and work up to TAM, as it presents a more compelling story as to the importance of investor funding, and to the potential growth of the startup.

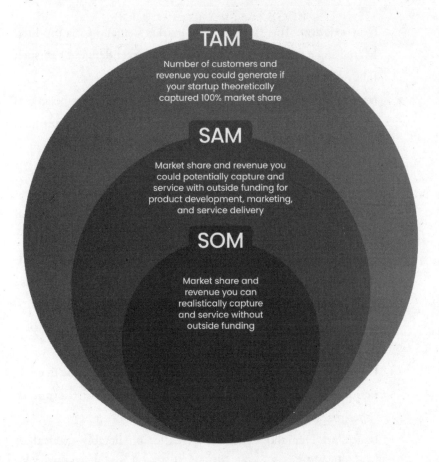

TAM

Number of customers and revenue you could generate if your startup theoretically captured 100% market share

SAM

Market share and revenue you could potentially capture and service with outside funding for product development, marketing, and service delivery

SOM

Market share and revenue you can realistically capture and service without outside funding

Market Analysis—Understanding Your Market

Standardized and defensible market data increases confidence and reduces risk for you and your investors. After identifying your market, you need to understand your market. While this may sound like a boring academic exercise, it's extremely important! "Market demand type" identifies the product demand in your serviceable addressable market (SAM) based on the level of supply, competition, and consumer demand. Your go-to-market strategies will only work if built to match market demand.

There are eight commonly recognized market demand types:

- **Non-existing:** There's no current market demand for a product. Marketing a product to a non-existing market demand can spell failure if the market doesn't respond.

- **Negative:** There is product supply, and the product is beneficial to consumers, but the market is rejecting the product. A product may become obsolete or overtaken by newer technology, or it may not be pleasurable, such as dental treatment or surgery.

- **Unwholesome:** There's demand for a product, but the product is detrimental to the customer, like opioids or illegally pirated intellectual property.

- **Latent:** Customers don't yet know they have demand for a product but will once the product is marketed or after they purchase it. New and novel products, like smartphones and their associated technologies, like text messaging, were an example of a latent demand.

- **Declining:** Market demand is declining. This may be due to competition, new technologies making an older product irrelevant, or other market forces, like inflation.

- **Irregular:** Demand exists but is either predictably cyclical or unpredictably rising and falling. This is okay for startups who supply seasonal products, like holiday decorations or seasonal clothes, but this can be dangerous for a startup reactively throttling marketing and production to meet an unpredictably irregular market demand.

- **Full:** Demand is fully met by the supply. This is ideal for startups already servicing the market.

- **Overfull:** The demand exceeds the supply. Startups cannot meet the market demand. There is risk for startups that grow rapidly to meet an overfull demand, who then find themselves too large when the market demand falls off or supply increases due to competitors.

To identify your market demand type, I recommend industry reports or market report searches from IBISWorld or Statista.com. You can more directly evaluate market demand for your specific product by using limited Facebook or Google ad tests within your target market for Google trend keyword searches aligned to your product. You can also utilize web aggregators, which make it easier to find businesses you want to research, since the aggregators have gathered businesses in one place. This can be beneficial when looking for brands to sell to, potential acquirers, competitors, and so forth.

Revenue Growth Drivers and Competitive Market Share Percentage

Revenue growth drivers describe how you plan to generate revenue within your serviceable obtainable market (SOM) or serviceable addressable market (SAM), given that you'll likely have competition. Which growth driver path will you take to win market share?

The competitive market share percentage measures the size and prevalence of your company in its respective industry. What percent (if any) of your SAM is already being serviced by your competitors, and how is your startup measuring up? This can be measured as a percent of revenue or percent of customer base.

Annual Contract Value

Annual contract value (ACV) is the average amount of revenue your startup makes from a single contract/customer over the course of a year. If you're already generating revenue from your product, then you calculate your ACV by dividing your twelve-month revenue by the number of unique customers in that twelve-month period.

Founders who don't yet have revenue can forecast ACV using average product price. To get this, you have to rely on your ideal customer profile and customer persona, which is the persona of the person you are selling to at a business, in a business-to-business (B2B) transaction, or the actual customer in a business-to-customer transaction. You also need to understand your competition and the prices at which they are selling—this will give you the acceptable range.

Once you gather the prices of your competitors, you will want to be above or underneath the average price, depending on what you are optimizing for. If you are optimizing for price, you will have a lower price. If you are optimizing for service and quality, you will price your product(s) higher. Therefore, if you are after people with little disposable income, you will optimize for price, but if you are after people who have a lot of disposable income, you will optimize by service and quality. It all depends on who your customers are and with whom you are going to compete.

Don't overcomplicate your ACV calculations. This is a very early estimate, and you may not have all the data necessary to be extremely precise. Document all assumptions used to calculate your ACV (or any calculations you make early in your startup days) so you can explain your results to investors. Be realistic. Base your numbers on what looks probable in your industry for a new business, based on a number of other companies. By itself, ACV isn't a super-useful metric. However, coupled with accurate market sizing, ACV yields valuable advisory board insights. But how do you determine the size of your target market?

Cost of Acquiring a Customer

Average market cost of acquiring a customer is also referred to as the customer acquisition cost (CAC). CAC spreads the costs of advertising, tools used for sales and marketing, and the salaries paid to employees directly involved in sales and marketing across the total number of customers who purchased your products.

Calculating industry-wide CAC is challenging, but you can generally find a few different estimates through Internet searches. Large publications, like *Forbes*, or industry-specific websites, often have articles that include industry CAC estimates.

Average Customer Lifetime Value

Average customer lifetime value (LTV) is the average revenue you and your competitors can expect to generate from a single customer over the course of that customer's relationship with your startup. Comparing the LTV to CAC helps you forecast revenue and helps you balance where you allocate resources.

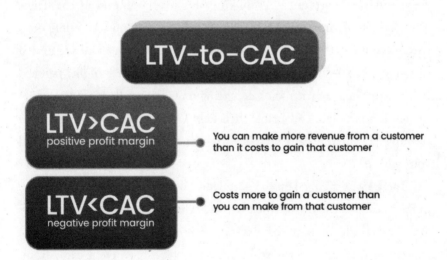

Early in a startup's lifecycle, CAC and LTV are broad estimates to help you estimate valuation, revenue potential, and how much money to raise. As a startup approaches breakeven and prepares for rapid, large-scale growth, optimizing the LTV-to-CAC ratio is critical to creating favorable revenue margins and growth.

All of these forecasted numbers become easier to gauge once you have been in business for a while and can fill in real numbers to compare with your estimates.

Startup and Product "What" and "Why"

As Simon Sinek, author of *Start with Why*, says, "Very few people (or startups) can clearly articulate why they do what they do." That's why it is imperative that you can clearly articulate what your startup does, and why, as well as what, the product does and why it exists.

To give you an "over the edge" example of how I learned the importance of what and why, let me return to my El Capitan experience. Remember, this is the largest solid granite rock face in the world, and three thousand feet tall . . . making this a very imposing challenge. Therefore, I planned ahead carefully and focused my attention on a specific route—"the nose"—until I could close my eyes and see myself reaching for handholds. It wasn't until late on the first night, perched halfway up the majestic rock face, sitting on what is called a "portaledge" (which is basically a collapsible shelf held up by ropes, big enough for a sleeping bag), that I really saw the importance of knowing your what and your why.

There I was, wedged on the portaledge, over a thousand feet in the air, in the middle of the night, when "nature called." So I checked my harness and shuffled off the portaledge to take care of business. If you know the expression "pissing into the wind," this is obviously where it came from. The only problem was the wind was blowing up the rock face toward me. At this point, I was plastered against the side of one of the most majestic mountains in the world getting pee all over my clothes.

If that weren't bad enough, as I slowly started back, I gave the safety rope attached to my harness a quick tug for reassurance—and felt it slip. I had checked my harness carefully before I clambered off the portaledge, but, like an idiot, I had not checked that the rope my harness was actually attached to was properly anchored. As I stood there, in damp clothing, six very long feet away from the portaledge, the rope slid all the way loose, and I realized I was one misstep away from tumbling to my death. This really brought into perspective two very important questions: What am I doing and why am I doing this?

In a startup, you are always on a narrow shelf, and more often than not, you have near-death experiences getting past these points. Therefore, it is important, not just for you but for your team, partners, customers, and investors, to understand the what and the why. It's not only useful in stressful situations, but it basically serves as a guardrail keeping everyone in lockstep. And, like rock climbing, you are all on the same rope. So, all of you, and the fate of your startup, will survive (or not) together.

Let me give you another example in a more familiar business setting. I was recently on a board call where I witnessed a group of investors arguing with a founder who was going over the next steps of the startup. The investors were growing frustrated, thinking that the startup had taken a pivot that they did not know about, which created a delicate and stressful situation. However, I had previously instructed the founder to create a "what and why" from the beginning of the startup, so the founder was prepared and able to pull that up, address the concerns of the investors, and show the group that this was, indeed, in the original plan. In fact, the founder was able to show details of his North Star creating realignment!

Although there was a disruption, the investors ultimately conveyed that they appreciated the exercise, and it gave them confidence in the direction the startup was taking. Since then, I have encouraged founders to display the what and the why of their North Star on the first slide of every board deck to ensure that there is never any reason to waste valuable time addressing confusion that could be avoided with the proper preparation!

Product What Statements

Your "product what statement" explains what your specific products provide for your customers. You will create what statements for each of your products and services. These statements facilitate in-depth conversations about your products. They'll also assist your investor communications, inform your market identification, and you'll use them when building your ideal customer profile.

PRODUCT "WHAT" STATEMENT

Product Name uses

Descriptions and Features

to **Benefits received**

EXAMPLE
The Halo Drone system uses all-weather technology that saves lives and money

You'll frequently leverage your product what statements during pitches and brief conversations, to succinctly and accurately explain your startup and product(s) to a broad audience, who may not have knowledge of your industry or intent.

At this point, you've identified and analyzed your target market and competitors, and you've codified your startup and product what statements.

You'll now compose your startup and product *why* statements, as in, *why* does your startup exist? Why will your customers buy specific products? And how does your startup and its products benefit your customers?

Startup What Statements

Your startup's what statement explains what your startup does, what *need* it fills, and prompts what products you make. Startup what statements look at your startup as a whole entity, beyond the products you manufacture and/or sell. These statements are meant to prompt the question "what do you make?" This is a question you want your listener to ask. Unlike your product, which is an outcome of your startup, the startup what statement is the catalyst of the vision. It's a story to capture the interest of the listener.

In previous chapters, you read about my story. I started with nothing and ended up with something. You will now compose your startup what statement, as in: What does your startup do? How did you get the idea? This is your way of leading them to ask about the products and/or services you sell. But it's more than that. It's what your business is all about and how it came to be. At conferences, investor pitches, and seminars, talking about the influence of your Aunt Faye or your grandfather is part of your startup what statement, as in: What problems does your startup solve? What does your startup stand for?

If I am talking about my most recent startup as a business designed to help founders avoid ending up as one of the many failed startups, I would talk about *what* my motivation is, such as, to help change the world's big problems, like environment, sustainability, inclusion, and wealth inequality, through helping founders by making it easier to start a business and be successful. You can see the difference between the *product* what and the *startup* what. My products are the books and the Visionaries platform; my startup what answers what problems I want to attempt to solve, as noted above.

The formula is simple:

1. **Acknowledge a problem/opportunity:** If you've had exposure to the startup world, you have already heard the question "What problem are you solving?" It's a very common phrase in our space. However, there is also another side that most people miss. What opportunity are you taking advantage of? It's true that a problem in the mind of an entrepreneur is an opportunity. In this case, we are separating them. A problem, in this case, is a real problem, such as the tons of plastic in the oceans. It's a pain point, a broken process that, if not addressed, will become a serious threat to our environment. When I was doing a 525-mile bicycle ride from San Francisco to Los Angeles, there was a very long, highly traveled section of the bike paths with no place to get water, requiring riders to take a road twenty miles out of the way to a convenience store, just to get some water. The person I rode with said, "Look at all these people going to the same place just to get a water refill. That's a missed opportunity for a water refill station." If you are a visionary founder, I bet you don't miss many opportunities.

    There is a nuance in the idea of the problem presenting an opportunity. This is a *need*. What your company is doing is filling a need with a product versus solving a problem. The catalyst of the product is your startup what.

2. **Feature:** The feature refers to the specific parts of the problem or opportunity. Our business could be one that offers riders on the highly populated bicycle route from San Francisco to Los Angeles convenient, easily accessible water refilling stations along the lengthy stretches where there is no water. You see, at this point, we do not talk about the water, the container, or the type of service, but the reason the startup exists in the first place. It's the step before the product. It's what problem you are trying to solve.

3. **Benefit:** Think what the real benefits are. The most obvious one is the convenience, but that is a feature. How is convenience a benefit? Riders no longer have to ride twenty miles off the trail, deal with traffic, lock up their bike, and stand in line, smelling like a horse, to buy the water, then ride back to the path using the very water they just filled. The real benefit is not having lost time, lost energy, and the embarrassment of smelling like a horse. On all three of the above, the way I teach this is to have founders start with single words on a whiteboard, then simply stuff the rest. Now, let's use the larger problems I am trying to solve with StartupScience.io.

Problem/Opportunity

1. **Wealth inequality.** Wealth inequality is real. The top 1 percent of households in the United States hold more than 30 percent of the country's wealth.
2. **Income inequality.** Income inequality is evident, as the majority of people are living paycheck-to-paycheck, according to data from the Federal Reserve.
3. **Inclusion.** Consider reports from the Federal Reserve on wealth inequality through the lens of the racial wealth gap, indicating that "the average Black and Hispanic or Latino households earn about half as much as the average White household and own only about 15 to 20 percent as much net wealth."
4. **Environmental issues.** Environment is about cleaning up the mess humans have recklessly created. The World Health Organization has measured concentrations of toxin swell over two times above the recommended limit, and Andean glaciers, which provide vital water resources for millions of people, are shrinking, and there is an increase in the intensity and frequency of extreme weather events.

5. **Sustainability.** Sustainability is a concept reflecting the principle that we must meet the needs of the present without compromising the ability of future generations to meet their own needs. Startup founders, such as Pat Brown, CEO of Impossible Foods, which develops plant-based substitutes for meat products, and Cara Nicoletti, whose Seemore Meats & Veggies produces carbon-neutral, vegetable-forward sausages, are changing the world; they are not large companies caught up in the public markets capital trap.

An Example of a Startup What Statement

Problem—StartupScience.io is committed to supporting and advancing business solutions that contribute to some of the world's most pressing social and environmental challenges, in sectors and thematic areas that include the environment, clean energy, health, food security, water, national security, and the Global Sustainability Goals.

Feature—Empowering a diverse range of founders, including underserved populations. We do this through accessibility to education, tools, and resources, and the visionary's platform, offering all founders a path to solving our world's most pressing issues.

Benefit—Founders change the world, and StartupScience.io's mission is to help them improve the world and everything on it for generations.

Startup Why Statements

Your startup and product why statements will also help you build your ideal customer profile, and communicate with your investors, while guiding your product development and informing your go-to-market strategies.

This statement explains why you started developing your startup in the first place, and how it will benefit your customers. Founders would be wise to be prepared to answer the following questions, which, with permission, were given to me by a friend and incredibly intelligent neurodivergent Stanford fellow, best-selling author Gregg Horowitz.

- Why this problem and solution?
- Why me? Why am I the right person or team to solve this problem? (This is where the subject matter expert comes in.)
- Why now? (This is about timing, as in, "Why is this time the right time?")

To help you with this, I personally like the old strengths, weaknesses, opportunities, and threats (SWOT) method. It's simple, easy to understand, flexible, and is a multi-tool. A SWOT analysis is an honest assessment of the target of the SWOT, in this case, your startup. For each category, you'll list three to five single words or short phrases.

Strengths, Weaknesses, Opportunities, Threats Quad Chart

Be honest about where your startup is today. Avoid wishful thinking about where you hope to be.

It's a common practice to plot your SWOT on a quad chart, as shown here.

Sample SWOT Analysis
For a Startup's Product

Internal to what you're assessing

Strengths
- Proven technology
- Easy-tp-use
- Redundant operation

Weaknesses
- Complex design
- Fragile materials
- Easily replicated

Opportunities
- Emerging technologies
- Dropping material costs
- Clear customer requirements

Threats
- Growing security risks
- Rising material costs
- Pending regulation changes

External to what you're assessing

With your startup SWOT complete, you'll now identify what *problem* your startup is solving for its customers. Be specific. If feasible, include whether your startup helps its customers make money or save money.

Here's an example:

First, what is the problem you want to address to meet the needs of your customers?

Problem: "Slow or nonexistent emergency response for hikers in challenging terrain and weather that may lead to unnecessary permanent disability or death. Training for high-risk emergency response is also costly and prone to injuries."

Next, what *solutions* does your startup offer to address the customers' problem?

"Company X offers emergency response agencies and hikers a suite of on-demand, drone-based solutions to provide medical assistance regardless of weather or terrain."

Finally, what *impact* does your startup's solution have on its customers?

"Company X saves emergency response startups costly training time, saves money by reducing manpower requirements, and reduces risk to emergency responders, while saving lives."

Now, combine your SWOT and your problem, solution, and impact statements into a single startup why statement:

"Company X leverages decades of rescue and drone experience to reduce training time and manpower costs, and decreases risk for emergency responders and hikers, with a suite of on-demand, all-weather, all-terrain, drone-based emergency response solutions."

Product Why Statements

You will now repeat the same process to develop a *product* why statement. While you may have several products or services, you'll only create one product why statement, unless your various products target different industries or markets.

However, you'll want to repeat a SWOT analysis for each product you offer. Remember, strengths and weaknesses are internal to your products. Opportunities and threats are external.

Compose your problem, solution, and impact statements, and then merge them into a single product why statement.

"Company X's system uses advanced sensors, connectivity, and payload technologies to save time, money, and lives, with on-demand, all-weather, and all-terrain emergency medical response."

Your product why statement tells your startup, customers, and potential investors why your product will succeed, and why it aligns with the needs of your market. It also informs your product development road map and investments.

Ideal Customer Profile

Now you shift from your startup and products to those who will be purchasing what you sell. You must have a very clear picture of who your customers will be, in order to tailor your sales and marketing to them.

Your ideal customer profile (ICP) is where you identify the profile of customer accounts/buyers who benefit from your product and require affordable sales, marketing, and services to convert and retain. The ICP summarizes the characteristics of the ideal customer within your serviceable obtainable market (SOM) and serviceable addressable market (SAM). As part of your North Star, your ICP also serves as a constant guiding principle for critical steps throughout the forthcoming phases of the Startup Science Lifecycle, like product development and go-to-market (GTM) strategies.

Once you're done with your ICP, your ideal customer should seem like a personal friend . . . someone you know very well. In fact, Steve Jobs used to say, "Get closer than ever to your customers. So close that you tell them what they need to know well before they realize it themselves."

Whether you intend to market your product to other businesses (B2B), or direct to consumers (B2C), it's critical that your ICP:

1. Is not overly broad.
2. Resides 100 percent within your serviceable addressable market.
3. Aligns with the customer base of companies that may acquire you in the future.

You'll create your ICP by answering specific questions about your potential customers. This culminates in an ICP statement, which is typically a single sentence that narrowly describes the most important characteristics of your ideal customer profile.

You will then accomplish a SWOT analysis of your ideal customer, just as you did for your startup and your product(s).

Remember, strengths are characteristics internal or unique to your ideal customer. For example, if developing an ICP for a B2B client, strengths may include "experienced," "cash-rich," and "has dedicated customers." For a B2C startup, strengths for an ideal customer may be "tech-savvy," "confident," and "motivated to buy."

Weaknesses are also internal to your ideal customer. For a B2B client, weaknesses may be "aging equipment," "slow processes," and "frequent cash-flow issues." A B2C ideal customer's weaknesses may be "easily distracted" and "highly reliant on customer support."

Opportunities and threats are *external* to your ideal customer. For a B2B ideal customer, opportunities could be "expanding market" and "new technologies." For a B2C ideal customer, opportunities could be "new mobile device" and "successful investments."

Finally, threats for a B2B ideal customer may be something like "new competitors" and "new regulations." And for a B2C ideal customer, "potential job loss" and "makes risky investments."

With our SWOT analysis complete, we've started to piece together an initial image of our ideal customer. You will need to continue narrowing down the definition of your ideal customer.

If you'll sell your product to businesses as a B2B, you'll identify facts about your ideal business client, such as:

- Their industry
- Number of employees
- Annual revenue
- Their reach—global, national, regional

The picture of your ideal customer is becoming clearer. Now, you'll tie your ideal customer to your product and services.

If you'll sell directly to consumers, then you'll list ideal customer demographic characteristics, such as:

- Age
- Income
- Gender
- Location

By purchasing your product, does your ideal customer seek to make money or save money? Sometimes it's tough to quickly answer this question, especially when selling direct to consumers. But motivations are almost always resolved to one of those two options.

If your product or service appears to save your customers time, then carry that outcome one step further. What will they do with that extra time as it relates to making or saving money?

Next, how specifically will they use your product to achieve their goal? Maybe your product helps a company streamline a process, which saves them money. Maybe your new software helps end users commute faster, saving them time, increasing their productivity, and therefore, making them money.

Finally, let's list the primary problems your ideal customer faces that your product addresses. A business might be utilizing outdated warehouse management software, or an end user may always be losing their public transportation tickets.

Once you've gathered a lot of information about your ideal customer, you will need to consolidate your answers into a single, brief ICP statement that summarizes who they are and what they're looking for in the context of your product.

Now you will write your ideal customer profile statement, such as:

"My ideal customer is a mid-sized US-based janitorial startup that needs to improve their cleaning supply acquisition process to reduce frustration and save money."

Remember, your ideal customer profile will focus your entire startup's efforts toward beneficial customer growth. Be methodical and confident in developing your ideal customer profile statement, and about being obsessed with growing the right customer base.

Customer Stories and Buyer Personas

This is where you identify the buyers within your ICP accounts and their wants, needs, and current means for addressing them to achieve "product-market fit" (PMF), which essentially means developing a product that your buyers will buy and use.

You've identified your ideal customer profile. But you're likely not the only startup targeting customers in that ideal customer profile. How will you differ from your competitors? What customer needs do you meet that your competitors do not meet?

Identifying your ICP doesn't necessarily tell you the various *reasons* customers within your ICP would want to use your product. It'll be difficult identifying how you'll excel over your competitors without knowing how your product solves the various problems faced by your customers. To address these questions, you'll identify your startup's company competitive advantages and combine that with your ideal customer profile to develop ICP user/customer stories.

Customer vs. User

For some companies, their customers may not be the end user of their product. This may be the case for business-to-business companies selling Software as a Service (SaaS) products. For this course, we'll use the terms "customers" and "users" interchangeably.

But be aware, if your customers and end users are different, then you may need to create separate company competitive advantages and user/customer stories for each.

Company Competitive Advantages

Your company competitive advantages (CCAs) compare what your customers need and value to areas in which your startup can compete and excel over competitors. This means researching your competition closely.

Determining your CCAs early on helps you design your startup structure, product features, sales and marketing, service delivery, and support, based on the expectations of customers within your ICP.

By recognizing advantages you have over your competitors early in the Vision phase, you can later focus your efforts and funding on areas such as quality, volume, or speed that customers in your ICP will expect, and that can set you apart from your competitors. You will also avoid wasting time, money, and effort on features or support that your customers won't expect and don't need.

To develop your CCAs, start by using a short sentence, identifying the primary customer *needs* that your product or service addresses.

Frame this from the customer's perspective. For example: "I need a more efficient and affordable inventory tracking tool." Try to identify at least two such customer needs.

Next, list specific *cost advantages* you offer (or plan to offer) your customers, which align with their primary needs. Cost advantages include (but are not limited to):

- Pricing
- Contract structures
- Discounts
- Referral incentives

Now, consider what *conveniences* you offer your ideal customer, which align with their primary needs.

Conveniences include (but are not limited to):

- Service and support
- Human assistance
- Product's ease of use

Next, identify how your ideal customer measures *excellence* in the products they purchase and the vendors they choose. Excellence includes (but is not limited to):

- Quality
- Volume
- Speed

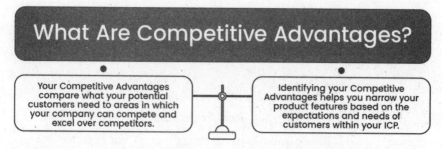

Now, considering your customers' needs, explain how your startup and product deliver, or will deliver, excellence in each area valued by your ICP.

Based on what your ideal customer needs and values (quality, volume, speed), and *your ability* to compete in those areas, you will then be able to choose the areas in which you want to compete in order to excel over your competitors.

For example, Apple is not focused on price. Instead, quality and ease of use are clearly the focus. Amazon is all about price and ease of use, while FedEx is focused primarily on service.

Consider your priorities and available resources. For example, you may need to prioritize excelling in quality instead of volume, if volume is only a minor consideration for your ideal customers.

Now, identify areas in which your ideal customer would, or would not, pay more for your product (or a similar product). What do they value enough to pay extra?

For example, will your ideal customers pay more for quality of product (over-engineered versus sufficient)? Areas to consider include (but are not limited to):

- Quality
- Volume
- Speed
- Customer service

Next, list features of your product (if any) that may be easier and cheaper for your ideal customer to do on their own. For example, if your product contains a database structure similar to Google Sheets, but adds no other benefit or product integration for the customer, then it would be easier and more affordable for them to use Google Sheets.

Now you'll identify reasonable and unreasonable demands and expectations. What demands or expectations could you have of your customers that they would consider unreasonable?

For example, it's *unreasonable* for me to ask users to reenter their personal information when setting up their account after they just provided the same information when purchasing my product.

But it's *reasonable* for me to ask customers to commit to an annual contract for my product, based on account setup time and complexity.

Now reverse roles and list any demands or expectations your customers could have of you or your product that *you* consider unreasonable. For example, it's *unreasonable* for my customers to expect after-hours, live customer support. But it's *reasonable* for my customers to expect a free trial period prior to committing to an annual contract.

Next, describe any training or skills you think are necessary for your customers, to reduce your ongoing costs. For example, "It's important that users have some training or understanding of point-of-sale systems. This will reduce the volume of customer service calls and requests I receive."

Finally, consolidate any testimonials or feedback you've received (if any) from current or past customers. Provide direct quotes, if you are able, as this will be very compelling to investors.

Composing Ideal Customer Profile User/Customer Stories

Considering all the information you've provided, and your ideal customer profile statement, compose your ideal customer profile user/customer stories. These stories consider customer needs and expectations to provide a more targeted look at a variety of potential customers within your ICP. This helps you refine product features, marketing strategies, service delivery, and customer support methods.

Concise user/customer stories, accompanied by thorough research, increase confidence and reduce risk for you and your investors. Plus they help you identify the correct pool of early users (your "user advisory board"), and reduce your time to revenue.

When composing your user/customer stories, use the format:

"I work at [ICP company]. As a [persona/user], I want [to achieve this goal] so that I can have [this outcome]."

Here's an example:

"As a franchise temporary storage startup, I want to improve efficiency and ease of use of my inventory management system so I can improve employee efficiency and reduce lost sales opportunities due to inaccurate data."

Buyer Personas

So far, you've established your ecosystem (aka your startup universe), detailed your market, built your ideal customer profile, and determined user/customer stories based on your competitive advantages. This has narrowed your target market from potentially millions of customers to user/customer stories representing the general demographics, problems, and goals of a handful of simulated customers that reflect your overall ideal customers. You now know who your ideal customers are and what they care about as it relates to your product.

But to efficiently allocate your resources toward product development, go-to-market strategies, and customer support, you need a more focused understanding of *what motivates your potential customers* to become buyers.

It's important to remember, people buy products and services, not companies. Let me explain, as I have run into this so many times I have lost track. Something that is good for the company is *not* necessarily good for the people who work there, especially efficiencies. I have, on many occasions, done a great job with my ICP and not thought about the actual buyer. The thing you are selling could be forcing them to get it approved with someone, which can cause stress. You could be automating their job. You could create more work for them, less work for them, and so on.

When you think about a buyer persona, think like a person, not a company, because, again, more often than not, you will find what's good for the company is not good for your buyer. Learn them, learn about how your offering can reduce frustration and make their life easier. You need a "champion" to push this through, so think about them, because even if you have the best solution, you will not be able to get past that gatekeeper.

To gain this deeper understanding, you'll develop buyer personas, which are detailed descriptions of your target buyers' goals, priorities, influences, information sources, and how they measure success. Together, user/customer stories and buyer personas plot a *buyer* decision *road map* and are the beginning of your *buyer journey*, which helps you understand how to target product, sales, marketing, and support resources from a buyer's first exposure to your product, through purchase and retention.

Accurate personas are your key to successful product development and go-to-market strategies, which will be elaborated upon in the upcoming phases. The measurable outcome of successful buyer personas is that you generate three to five times more revenue from a buyer than you spend on sales and marketing to get that buyer's business.

To complete your buyer personas, you'll assess the goals, priorities, means, and metrics for each potential buyer persona. As with ideal customer profile and user story development, this analysis applies whether you sell to other businesses (B2B) and your buyer is an employee of that business, or whether you sell directly to consumers (B2C), and the buyer is the end user of your product.

First, we'll assess your buyer's goals. In developing your ideal customer profile statement, you identified goals of making or saving money.

For buyer personas, you can assess other, potentially more personal goals besides just those two. If you sell to other businesses, and your buyer is an employee who will make or inform the decision to buy your product, then their personal goals may be a *promotion, raise,* or *job retention*.

If you sell directly to consumers, then your buyer, as the end user of your product, may want to *lose weight* or *order food more efficiently*.

Now, we'll identify your potential buyer's priorities. If selling B2B, then your buyer's priorities are their professional responsibilities based on their job and the needs of their business.

For example, if they're the chief operations officer for their company, then their priorities may be to *streamline operations* and *reduce wasted resources*.

For a B2C buyer, their priorities may align with their family, work, or hobby. If a consumer is responsible for preparing food for their family, then their motivation for purchasing your product could be to *save time and money* within those responsibilities. Priorities may not always be different from their goals.

Next, list your buyer's means. These are the tools and resources at their disposal to accomplish their goals and priorities. While money, employees, and software are obvious means, we also need to consider how your buyers gather information to inform their purchasing decisions.

I call these various informational platforms "watering holes." Some examples include:

- YouTube
- Podcasts
- Blogs
- Platforms (social media, websites)
- People (mentors, advisors)
- Events (webinars, trade shows)
- Any other sources they use that will give you insight into how best to gain their business

A consumer's means, for example, may be to reference Amazon product reviews prior to purchasing. That's critical data toward helping you develop your personas and marketing strategies.

Finally, we'll assess what metrics or measures your buyers use to gauge progress toward their goals or priorities. For B2B, an employee may use *internal financial* or *service delivery metrics* to assess priorities, and *leadership feedback* or *personal performance reports* to measure their personal goals.

A consumer end user may use *progress in their personal hobby* to measure personal goals and measure *family satisfaction with meals* as metrics toward meeting their priorities.

Now we'll combine your goals, priorities, means, and metrics into several short, two-sentence buyer personas.

Use the format: "I'm a **[job, personal title, or demographic description]** who uses **[means]** to achieve **[goals]** and **[priorities]**. I measure progress toward my goals and priorities with **[metrics]**."

Here is an example of a buyer persona:

> "I'm the **CIO at Acme, Inc.** and I use **weekly team meetings and *Forbes* podcasts** to **help me improve communication with our customers** and **to increase my position within the company.** I measure progress toward my goals and priorities by reading **customer complaint reports and job performance feedback sessions.**"

Because most startups lack the resources to successfully market to multiple buyer personas, we'll combine your individual buyer personas into one single, unified buyer persona, which will merge the characteristics from your individual buyer personas that most represent the majority of your serviceable addressable market (SAM). This unified buyer persona will be the template from which you will form your initial product test and go-to-market strategies.

An accurate unified buyer persona allows startups to more efficiently use resources, reduces investor risk, and increases your chance of a successful go-to-market campaign. You're likely not the only startup targeting customers in that ideal customer profile. Other companies have likely profiled similar customers. Therefore, in order to create your buyer personas, you must be able to clearly answer two questions: How will you differ from your competitors? What customer needs do you meet that your competitors can't? To answer these questions, you'll need to research your competitors and identify your company's competitive advantages. Then you'll combine that with your ideal customer profile to develop your ideal customer profile user/customer stories. These stories show why this is the ideal customer *and* what you offer them that your competitors do not. Identifying customers and finding a clear advantage over your competitors is like finding gold.

CHAPTER WRAP-UP

Yes, this chapter was long, and it's only the first part of Phase One. It does, however, provide the foundation for the phases to come. We focused on vision, North Star, ecosystem, market identification and analysis, revenue growth drivers, and posed the all-important questions: What does your startup do? And why? We also focused attention on identifying your all-important ideal customer. We then looked at competitive advantages and how you can benefit from using a SWOT analysis. All of these areas will play key roles in the phases ahead. This is, as noted above, the foundation for building a successful startup. If there is one chapter to read again (I know it's long), *this* is it.

Phase One (Part 2): Focusing on the Endgame

In the world of business, the rearview mirror is always clearer than the windshield. Focusing on the end game, as the ultimate goal, is what separates the truly successful from the rest. Don't get distracted by short-term fluctuations; keep your eye on the long-term prize.

–Warren Buffett

If you've ever watched a suspense movie, or whodunit, or read such a book, here's a spoiler alert—most often the screenwriter, or author, knows who the culprit is from the start. As journalist Lisa Swan wrote in an article for Think-human.com, Matthew Weiner, creator of the popular TV show *Mad Men*, knew how the show would end down to the last shot. Lisa adds that "many authors write the endings of books first, before they get going with the beginning." That is what is known as beginning with the end in mind, and it is not just a force in creating art. Begin with the end in mind is the second habit of Stephen Covey's legendary book *The 7 Habits of Highly Effective People*.

Once you have identified your vision and North Star, as well as analyzed the marketplace and identified your ideal customer, you will need to focus your attention on how all of the above pertains to your exit and, more significantly, your ideal acquirer.

The US Department of Commerce has reported that only 20 percent of the startups that are for sale will successfully transfer hands to another owner. You might be an optimist and believe that, if you build a valuable startup, someone will eventually come along and buy it. But failing to formulate a path and plan for eventual acquisition will lower your exit value, cause missed exit opportunities, reduce how much money you can make from an exit, and even scare away investors.

Remember, the Startup Science Lifecycle path is designed to take you from Vision through Exit. Although counterintuitive, before you've earned your first customer, or even built your product, it's very important to consider your exit and to whom you will possibly sell. But first, we need to understand the basics of why one entity may want to purchase another.

Acquisition Motivations

The motivations for an acquirer to purchase a business generally come down to *making money* (top of the profit and loss sheet) or *saving money* (bottom of the profit and loss sheet). There's frequently a mix of both factors, but one is usually a higher priority for an acquirer. These methods are also tied to the balance sheet and/or the profit and loss statements, as the acquisition will affect one or both. Top-line revenue will affect the P&L, while margin affects bottom-line profits. In my personal experience, selling to an acquirer who seeks profit is less beneficial, because you are not selling the "upside," and more or less, the business is what it is. Whereas other transaction types have some elements of "open ocean," the idea that there could be more with the help of the acquirer. In either case, an acquirer can be sold the benefits; however, the pure revenue-based deal leaves you with less elbow room to sell the hype.

With those two motivations in mind, we'll categorize acquisitions as either financial or strategic.

In a *financial acquisition*, the acquirer is purchasing a business based solely on the current value that purchase brings—usually from the revenue or profit the company generates, or the market share the company could bring to the acquirer. The acquirer is only considering the current value of the company, not any future value the company brings.

To decide whether to pursue a financial acquisition, acquirers will use the *absolute revenue growth* (how much more money this startup made this year compared to last year), and *revenue growth* as a percentage (by what percent the business revenue grew over the past year).

It's critical to note that an acquirer will only value growth that aligns with their own customers. This is called attachment. Your acquirer also has an ideal customer profile. If your growth doesn't align with your acquirer's ideal customer profile, then you're likely lowering the value of your business. Therefore, you'll want to know what percentage of your potential acquirer's customers have purchased your product. This is called attachment *rate*. The higher it is, the more likely your potential acquirer will be interested in buying your startup—after all, you already share customers. Acquirers prefer financial acquisitions because they can pay a lower purchase price than what the future value of the acquisition will bring them.

For example: if Startup A has an annual revenue of $500,000, then Company X may offer to purchase Startup A for $1,500,000 (a 3x multiple of the startup's revenue), even though Company X estimates it will increase its revenue by $5M within two years of the acquisition.

Financial acquisitions have the potential to limit the amount founders and investors can make when they sell their company.

In a *strategic* acquisition, the acquirer is purchasing a startup based on the future value the acquisition will bring them. For a strategic acquisition, acquirers primarily consider one of two factors:

1. The degree to which an acquirer can sell the startup's products to their customers and its own products to the customers of the startup they are acquiring.
2. And how much money the company's technology or process saves the acquirer. What's the bottom-line revenue value?

I recommend that founders and investors seek a strategic exit, as it tends to lead to larger exit prices, increasing the chances that an investor meets their target returns and that the founders will make a sizable amount of money.

Here's an example of one type of strategic acquisition: Startup A has a technology that can reduce Company X's operations costs by 35 percent. Over the course of five years, this savings increases Company X's bottom-line revenue by $250M. While Startup A currently has no customers, and is generating no revenue, Company X purchases Startup A for $60M based on the future value created from the operations savings.

Now that we know *why* acquirers purchase other companies, let's look at *what* an acquirer is actually purchasing when it acquires a company. There are three traditional exit transaction types:

1. In a stock purchase agreement (SPA), the acquirer purchases the entire company (all assets, revenue sources, expenses/debt, employees, etc.). They acquire all of the purchased company's assets.

2. In an asset purchase agreement (APA), the acquirer purchases only a product, technology, or process from another company.

3. An initial public offering (IPO) is when a private company issues public stock. This is, in essence, selling portions of a business to the public.

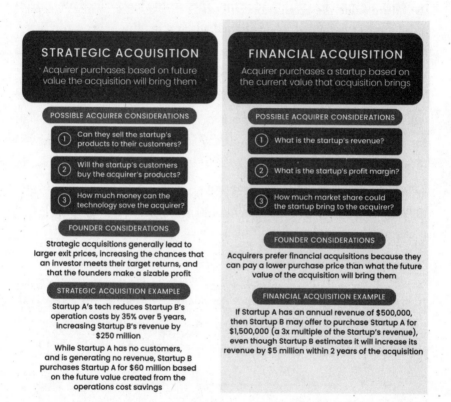

Understanding the transaction type your ideal acquirer is pursuing helps you align your business structure to their preferences. For example, if your acquirer tends to purchase entire companies, preferably startups (in a stock purchase agreement), then you know that features like the structure and operations of your functional areas, and your employee performance, will likely be important factors for your acquirer.

Valuation Drivers

Remember how my $25M mistake with Affiliate Traction stemmed from my ideal customer profile not aligning with my potential acquirer's ideal customer profile? My potential acquirer valued alignment (attachment) between my customer base and theirs. They would have valued my startup more if my customer base had aligned with theirs. But how do you determine what your potential acquirers will value from your business, and what do you do with that information?

Valuation is a belief, at a specific moment, of how much a business will be worth in the future. It's *not* necessarily the actual current value of the business, especially of a brand-new startup. Potential acquirers and investors use valuation as a tool to assess whether to purchase or invest in a business, and if so, for how much money. Valuation is driven by risk and uncertainty, what I call probability and predictability. Higher risk and uncertainty in a company will likely lower that company's valuation for investors and potential acquirers.

Early in a startup's lifecycle, *probability and predictability are uncertainty*, so risk is higher, and investor confidence is lower, driving a lower valuation. As a startup progresses through their lifecycle, uncertainty and risk should decrease, increasing investor confidence and increasing valuation.

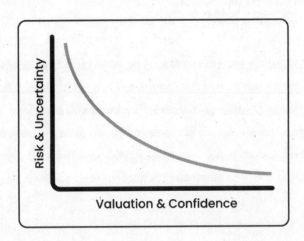

Remember, valuation for a startup is based on its potential future value. A startup declares a valuation to align with how much money they seek to raise from investors in a fundraising round. Setting the wrong valuation can decrease the likelihood of successful fundraising, reduce how much of the startup the founders own, or reduce the value of each portion of ownership. This is called dilution.

The "right" valuation is highly specific to where a startup is in the life-cycle, as well as the history of investments in similar companies in similar industries, and to each individual investor and potential acquirer.

The "right" valuation for a startup:

- Recognizes and accounts for the potential future value of the startup.
- Recognizes the uncertainty remaining in the startup.
- Allows founders and investors to obtain their desired reward upon exit.
- Provides room for the valuation to increase in the future, accounting for the fact that a startup will likely need to raise more money.

Defining Valuation Drivers

Valuation drivers are the metrics investors and acquirers look for to determine the value of your startup to them. Valuation drivers are the top of the key performance indicators (KPIs) stack that you will use to assign missions to your startup and to assess progress toward your exit.

Meaningful valuation drivers are measured within your ideal customer profile (ICP), which must align with the ICP of your potential acquirers.

There are four primary valuation drivers. We'll categorize each as either *internal* or *external* and *income* or *expense*, and associate them to functional areas within your startup, such as your product and engineering team, or sales and marketing team. This is the start of delegating specific KPI responsibilities to specific functional areas.

Internal drivers are directly measured from your startup's KPIs. External drivers require data from outside your startup. You'll use this outside data to make comparisons, and to align with a potential acquirer.

Let's look at the three primary valuation driver stacks, all of which can be measured by specific KPIs.

- **Growth** is an internal driver that indicates people like, and are using, your product, that the price is right, and that your go-to-market strategy was correct. It's validation that you're getting people to purchase your product and that it will continue. Growth is a function of your Sales and Marketing functional area.

- **Gross Margin** is an internal driver that indicates your product after costs is profitable, and you can safely take it to scale by increasing the size of your customer base. Gross margin is associated with Operations and Shared Services.

- **Retention** is an internal driver that shows the "stickiness" of your product. Solid retention indicates that people continue to like and use your product. Retention reflects the performance of your product delivery and is aligned with the service and support area.

Valuation drivers are the vital metrics that your investors will assess during funding rounds, and that your potential acquirers will assess when deciding to acquire your startup or your technology.

Failing to accurately target and measure valuation drivers, *aligned with your ideal acquirer's ideal customer profile and preferred exit type*, can reduce investor and acquirer confidence in your startup, or present them with an incomplete or inaccurate picture of your potential value. The more of your potential acquirer's valuation drivers you can meet, the higher your potential exit valuation, and the more money you can make as a founder.

Build Your Ideal Acquirer Profile

With an understanding of how and why businesses purchase other businesses, especially startups, and what valuation drivers they use, let's build your ideal acquirer profile and acquirer user/customer stories. We'll follow the same process we used to develop *your* ideal customer profile and user/customer stories.

Start by researching historical acquisitions of businesses that are *similar to yours*. You can use a resource like Crunchbase to identify the following characteristics about previous acquisitions:

- In what industry did the acquirer make an acquisition?
- What were the acquirer's annual revenue and cash reserves at the time of the purchase?
- Did the acquirer make a financial or strategic acquisition?
- Was their objective to make or save money?
- Was there customer alignment between the acquirer and the startup they purchased?
- How did that acquisition compare to the industry average for similar acquisitions?
- Are there any acquirers that stand out as having made frequent acquisitions of businesses that are startups similar to your startup?

With some baseline research out of the way, let's build your ideal acquirer profile starting with a SWOT analysis from the perspective of acquirers that may want to purchase your startup.

Remember, strengths and weaknesses are internal to your potential acquirer, such as their large capital reserves or aging fleet of vehicles. Opportunities and threats are external to your potential acquirer. This could include new technologies under development, product management, and/or pending government regulations.

Next, using your research, list key information and statistics about your ideal acquirer. This may take some more targeted Internet research about these acquirers. Look for interviews with company leadership, or vision statements about their future path.

Here are some examples:

- What was the acquirer's cash balance at the time of acquisition?
- How many employees do they have?
- What is their annual revenue?
- How many customers do they have?
- Who are their primary competitors?
- What are their needs? For example, do they need to expand their market share, or do they need to streamline operations to save money?

As you did with *your* ideal customer profile, you'll combine your acquirer's strengths, weaknesses, opportunities, and threats, plus the information data, into a single, concise, ideal acquirer profile statement.

Here's an example: "My ideal acquirer is a North American chemical distribution company with one thousand to five thousand employees, annual revenue of $30M to $100M, and more than $10M in cash reserves. They seek to expand their line of products and to rapidly grow their market share."

At this point, you may have a couple of potential acquirers in mind. That's great!

For your acquirer user/customer stories, you'll use the format: "As a **[type of Acquirer]**, I want to achieve **[objective]**, so that I can achieve **[desired outcome]**."

Here's an example: "As a multinational company looking to diversify my product line, I want to acquire other companies so I can sell their products to my customers, saving on product development costs and rapidly expanding my sales."

You can see how quickly and sharply your acquisition partner comes into focus.

With a clear ideal acquirer profile, several acquirer user/customer stories, and research into historical acquisitions of companies, including startups similar to yours, list several potential acquirer companies. You'll want to include:

- Company name.
- Number of customers.
- Percentage of shared ideal customer profiles.
- If you already have customers, how many of your customers are also their customers, and what percentage of your total customers are their customers (attachment rate).
- What average monthly and annual revenue they generate from each attached customer.
- Any common competitors, if any.
- Whether, if this company purchases you, they will use your product to make money off their current customer base or seek to expand into a new market using your product. For example, if you are selling to Pepsi and your product is another soda, they will be selling to their current customer base. However, if your product is a healthy drink, they will need to expand into a market that focuses on health drinks.
- Whether they would acquire your startup primarily to make money (increase top-line revenue) or save money (increase their bottom-line revenue).

The more refined, detailed, and researched description of why you're targeting specific acquirers, the more confidence you instill in investors, and the more impactful your valuation driver key performance indicator will be.

Your detailed ideal acquirer profile should include your ideal acquirer profile statements and acquirer user/customer stories. Creating a list of potential acquirers, based on your research and assumption behind this data, will be invaluable as you develop your product, set your go-to-market strategy, form your functional areas, and communicate with investors.

Remember, coming into a business that you are hoping to sell, and knowing as much about potential acquirers as possible, allows you to tailor all your startup plans, from products and customers to marketing to your ideal acquirer. This will make it easier to meet your end goal of an exit through a successful acquisition.

Build Your Exit Strategy

At this point, you should have a good idea of what your ideal acquirer looks like, their past acquisition behaviors, and what valuation drivers they value.

You'll now plot your exit strategy by setting a desired exit price, establishing your target acquisition timeline, and laying a time-based framework of key performance indicators, planning backward from your future exit, to where you are currently. These KPIs, which are designed to achieve your ideal acquirer's valuation drivers within your exit timeline, will form the basis of your startup's daily operations.

Setting an Exit Price

To set your desired exit price, start with your previous research to identify an average acquisition price for startups similar to yours.

You'll then need to make assumptions about what value your startup or product will add to your potential acquirer based on their valuation drivers and their preferred exit types.

If your ideal acquirer prefers financial acquisitions, then you'll need to forecast your annual revenue at your proposed exit time. If it's significantly higher than the average acquisition price you researched, then you can consider increasing your target exit price beyond the industry average.

You can estimate your future annual revenue by using your market sizing and annual contract value (ACV) work you previously accomplished. For example, you can use your serviceable obtainable market (SOM) revenue, or your SOM customer base multiplied by your ACV.

If your ideal acquirer prefers strategic acquisitions, then you will need to estimate the value you bring to that acquirer, besides your revenue. For example, your product or process may save your acquirer significant time and money in operating costs.

Depending on the industry, it's common to calculate your exit price using a *multiple* of the actual cost savings you bring. For example, if your software saves a startup $2M per year, it's not unreasonable to multiply that value by five to get an exit price of $10M.

Remember, your estimated exit price, calculated at this early phase (Vision), is not the current valuation of your startup. It's merely a rough estimate to guide the development of your KPIs, timelines, and how you plan your fundraising rounds. Within your startup, you'll frequently update this value throughout your Startup Science Lifecycle as your valuation becomes clearer. Of course, this is not information to share in the early stages of your development.

Next, estimate your desired exit timeline. For new startups, I recommend an exit timeline of three to five *years* from the start of the Vision phase. For more mature startups, this timeline can be reduced to as little as one to two years.

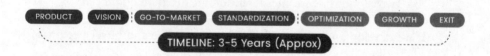

Create Your Ideal Acquirer Profile Statement

You can now add timeline and exit price into the ideal acquirer profile we wrote earlier.

"In three years, I will exit for $20M to a North American chemical distribution company with one thousand to five thousand employees, annual revenue of $30M to $100M, and more than $10M cash reserves that seeks to expand their line of products so they can rapidly grow their market share."

Mapping Key Performance Indicators

With a very rough estimate of your exit price and timeline, you'll now map KPIs aligned with your potential acquirer's valuation drivers—onto your timeline. This map moves back in time from exit, to profit, to product launch and your first sale, and finally to the present day. Let's take a look.

We know we want to exit in three years for $20M. Our Crunchbase research shows that our potential acquirer favored strategic exits based primarily on market share. The startups they have previously acquired had a high customer attachment rate and ideal customer profile alignment. They also valued year-over-year customer growth percentages higher than 50 percent and twelve-month customer retention greater than 60 percent.

So, to meet our ideal acquirer's valuation drivers, in three years we need to achieve the following valuation driver KPIs:

1. Customer attachment rate to our potential acquirer of at least 70 percent
2. Year-over-year customer growth rate of at least 50 percent
3. Twelve-month customer retention greater than 60 percent

If we develop an accurate ideal customer profile and buyer personas during our Vision phase, aligned with our ideal acquirer, then as we grow our customer base, it should automatically have a high attachment rate to our ideal acquirer. The goal is to make your startup as close to a perfect fit for the acquiring company as possible.

Let's work back from our exit to the present day. Year two to three is your year to grow your customer base with a focus on Sales and Marketing,

Service Delivery, and Customer Support functional areas. We can assign a valuation driver KPI to our sales and marketing team of 50 percent customer growth with a minimum of 70 percent attachment to our ideal acquirer profile. We'll assign the 60 percent, twelve-month retention KPI to our service delivery and customer support.

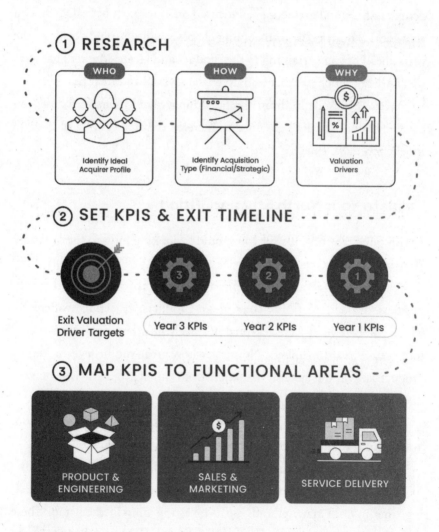

Even if you don't yet have any employees, you still need to map these KPIs into your timeline and associated functional areas. The time will come to hire your team to achieve these KPIs. But in the meantime, your investors must know that you have a high-fidelity plan with time-based KPIs designed to get you to exit.

Let's keep working backward. Year one to two is your year for product development and go-to-market KPIs, focused on getting your first customers with attachment to your acquirer. So, we'll need KPIs for product design, testing, and marketing, all focused on a customer base aligned with your ideal acquirer. The forthcoming chapters will illustrate details of the years ahead of you pertaining to the Product and Go-to-Market phases, as well as the other phases that lead up to the seventh and final Exit phase.

Your entire startup, from the beginning, should remain focused on achieving a broader KPI designed to increase the chances of a successful, timely, profitable exit.

Validate Your North Star and Vision

At this point, the first answer you should be looking for is to the question: Who will validate my ideas?

Validation is a form of confirmation, or affirmation, by others. In business, validation means your ideas, products, or services offered—which you believe in—are accepted positively by others, such as your customers and board members. No matter how great you believe an idea or product is, without honest validation from other people, it will be very difficult to get investors behind it.

At StartupScience.io, we use advisory boards for vision validation. You'll also lean on your advisory boards for product validation.

To kick-start the process of vision validation, you need to start talking to people. The people who help you refine your early ideas are investing time in your startup, and you're investing time in them too. These early conversations serve to foster relationships that you will grow in the months and years to come. The individuals who help validate your vision will likely become your first paying customers. These are the people who will tell you how you are doing so far and if they like your product enough to pay for it, or if they have concerns about it.

Put your ego aside, since you can't validate an idea by yourself without getting feedback from other people, and make necessary changes along the way, based on such feedback. Keep in mind that the people you talk with will have a wide range of ideas, some of which will be good, others not so much. Some people will actually help you fine-tune your concept, while others will nudge you to produce products that are more aligned with their needs. Consider how broad-based their ideas are. Also, look for repetition, or similarity, in the feedback you receive. If half a dozen people provide the same, or similar, comments, they may be on to something.

It's a healthy process. You need to be smart about who you choose for early-phase validation. If your validators push their own niche interests or have their own agendas, you might wind up building a startup that's perfect for them, but isn't scalable or sustainable in the broader marketplace, or doesn't appeal to companies you may seek to buy your startup.

You need to ask yourself if the people you're relying on to validate your vision are well aligned with the people you think will buy your product, or your startup.

Industry Advisory Board

An industry advisory board (IAB) should consist of subject matter experts and thought leaders in your target industry. Ideal IAB members are generally several layers removed from direct operations of a startup but have been in the industry for several years. Think of IAB members as "gray-haired" visionaries, who currently work *on* startups, not in startups. They likely won't be future customers of your product or service—especially if you sell your product directly to other startups.

Also keep in mind that this is not a check-the-box exercise or something you will outgrow. In fact, as your startup matures, you'll increasingly lean on your IAB to validate your strategic vision and to ensure you're prepared for each phase of maturity. You should meet formally with your IAB one or two times a year.

User Advisory Board (UAB)

Your user advisory board should be made up of approximately five to ten individuals you perceive will be the day-to-day users of your product or service. These are the people you built your product or service for and directly experience the benefits of your product or service. As with your IAB, you will repeatedly leverage your user advisory board for validation throughout the entire lifecycle of your startup.

Your user advisory board should directly align with the personas within your ideal customer profile. But as your product matures, it's likely your buyer personas will also mature and shift. What matters most is that your UAB is reflective of your actual users. Of course, as products and services change, your UAB may also have to evolve. At a minimum, you'll want to maintain active contact with your user advisory board every ninety days. This can be in the form of newsletters or personal emails. During certain critical times, such as prototyping and ideal acquirer profile product (see Phase Two—Product), you'll engage with your user advisory board more frequently, even weekly, to ensure accurate validation.

Continuous Validation

This is where you may engage accelerators, incubators, or universities. While it is not absolutely necessary that startups seek validation from startup assistance advisors, they do provide several benefits to founders.

Many founders see vision validation as a bit like a traffic signal. Hit a red light? Okay, there's more work to do. Yellow light? Fine, make some tweaks and get ready to roll. Green light? Thumbs-up, you're good to go, and you'll never look back.

Vision Validation

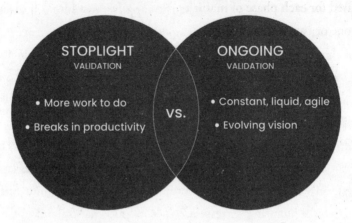

STOPLIGHT
VALIDATION

- More work to do
- Breaks in productivity

VS.

ONGOING
VALIDATION

- Constant, liquid, agile
- Evolving vision

Startup Assistance Advisors

This is where you may engage accelerators, incubators, or universities. While it is not absolutely necessary that startups seek validation from startup assistance advisors, they do provide several benefits to founders

The reality, however, is that vision validation should be a constant, liquid, agile, ongoing process. As your startup grows, your vision will evolve, and you'll need to keep actively examining and thinking about the stories you tell, the value you bring, and the people you serve. That agility is a big part of what StartupScience.io brings to the table.

Using this approach, you'll be constantly guided to revalidate and reinvigorate your ideas, to ensure your products and processes are properly aligned to the needs of your customers, your changing marketplace, and your eventual acquirer.

I've walked that path myself. In 2008, my startup Affiliate Traction was going gangbusters by promising to help retail e-commerce companies sell more of their product through online advertising—but when the bottom fell out of the economy, we had to rapidly pivot into a bear-market strategy focused on beating our competitors on price.

Such a radical change in approach is never easy to implement. But because we bit the bullet early on, and we were willing to toss out our existing vision *before* it failed, we were able to pivot early into a new approach calibrated to the new market reality. That meant we survived and ultimately thrived, even as many of our less nimble competitors failed.

Politicians often draw heat for flip-flopping, but I've never quite understood why. In the startup world, it's *good* to change your mind, as long as you're adapting in response to new information and not merely equivocating. A CEO who's still sticking to the vision they had a decade ago is stagnating, and their startup is probably suffering as a result. When you need to gain a better understanding of your target audience, you conduct audience research and create buyers.

When it comes to vision, the trick is to understand that believing in yourself doesn't mean ignoring external input that differs from your vision. Self-belief means believing you can execute on your vision, of course. But it also means the ongoing need to improve on your vision over time. The key to success in a startup, as in life, is to keep on evolving and moving forward—and to keep on validating, iterating, and revalidating your ideas as your startup grows.

Openly accepting feedback that challenges your core beliefs, no matter how uncomfortable, is a skill every successful founder must develop.

Presenting Your Vision for Validation–The Pitch

Your pitch should succinctly and clearly consolidate your vision and North Star elements to tell a compelling story about the minimum viable product ability of your vision and startup.

The objective in presenting your pitch depends on your audience. When pitching to your industry and user advisory boards, the goal is unbiased, honest feedback to refine your vision and North Star.

When pitching to investors, your goal is obviously to get funding. So, it's critical that you pitch to your advisory boards before pitching to investors. The more chances you have to pitch and refine your vision with your board members, the higher the likelihood of success with investors.

CHAPTER WRAP-UP

With your innovative idea validated, you're ready to turn your vision into a tangible product. Your North Star will become a living document that is recalibrated as your startup matures. From this point forward, your North Star is used to keep your startup on the most efficient and direct path toward exit. You'll stay engaged with your advisory boards, ensuring you understand your ICP's product requirements. And you're likely in a good position to raise pre-seed funding, so you can hire or contract a product and engineering team to build your prototype and minimum viable product (MVP). The average tech startup should be ready for the Product phase within six to twelve months of starting the Vision phase.

If you are interested in how more tactical experience courses can be found, please scan this QR code. You will also find best practices, templates, examples, suggested software, and startup incentives offered by the providers and how to get them.

Phase Two: Prototype and Product

> The MVP is the version of a new product which allows the team to collect the maximum amount of validation with the least cost and effort.
>
> **–Eric Ries, author of *The Lean Startup* and *The Startup Way*, books on modern founderial management**

I n Phase One (Vision) of the Startup Science Lifecycle, founders establish the vision and create the startup's North Star. Once this is completed, it's time to enter Phase Two (Product), where the refined vision and North Star turn into a product prototype.

Every startup should build a prototype and then a minimum viable product (MVP), which is validated by users. Sound easy? It's not in the least.

I'm a technophile with a fair amount of disposable income and a love of fast, futuristic, slightly madcap methods of transportation . . . electric sports cars. Hey, there are two parked in my garage. If Elon Musk ever gets the Hyperloop up and running, I'll be first in line to buy a ticket. I have already put a deposit down on space travel with World View, an exciting new startup I learned about on my *Startup Science Podcast.*

But there's one thing I've never owned, and that's a Segway. When they were launched, they were pitched to the public as the biggest transportation breakthrough since the internal combustion engine. By rights, I ought to have been their dream customer—but I never wanted one, and I certainly never bought one.

Why not? Well, Segway slipped up on a little thing called *product validation.* Their vision was fine. However, if they'd asked me, I would have explained that I loved the sound of a self-balancing electric vehicle that would make automobiles redundant, one that could whizz me through crowds at incredible speeds. But they fell short when it came to turning that vision into a real product that their target audience would actually buy and use.

Instead of revolutionizing personal transport, Segway produced oversized, heavy, expensive, and energy-hungry vehicles that even mobility nerds like me didn't want to buy. Segway's self-balancing scooters might have been packed with ahead-of-their-time technologies. But they were also bulky, impossible to take anywhere, hard to drive, even harder to park, and incapable of moving fast enough to make the whole thing worthwhile. Frankly, I'd rather ride my bike—and I wasn't the only one. Commuters spurned Segways, and today, they're mostly relegated to shunting security guards around shopping malls and tour guides with incredible insurance.

Misreading customers is one of the quickest ways to kill your startup, and according to CB Insights, it's implicated in up to 42 percent of startup failures. To avoid this, start with a prototype. Your prototype validates that you got the product right before you move on to the minimum viable product.

Definition of a Prototype

A prototype is a way to rapidly test the basic ideas and assumptions behind the product. In contrast, a minimum viable product is a *usable* version of the product with just the core feature or features, ideal for testing, resulting in feedback and useful data, yet with a minimum of time and money invested at this phase (Product). Prototypes ensure you don't build the next Segway.

Now in Phase Two (Product), it's time to prove that you can move from vision to product prototype and show your early-phase investors that you're capable of executing on the vision you've sold them, by building a real product prototype with which your customers will (hopefully) fall in love. You'll accomplish this by leveraging your advisory boards for product feature requirements, which are first tested internally via a lightweight prototype that you'll evolve into your minimum viable product. This iterative process increases investor confidence so that you'll be able to raise a round of funding to enter Phase Three: Go-to-Market.

The Significance of a Prototype

As Mark Twain once said, "Continuous improvement is better than delayed perfection"! I must say, in all my years, I have never seen any mistake more often than founders not getting the product in front of customers *before* it's done.

Imagine you're selling oatmeal cookies. Sure, you could bake five thousand cookies and pile them up in your store, but if it turns out nobody likes your recipe, you'll be left with thousands of unsold and unsellable cookies. Further, you'll have no ingredients left with which to try chocolate chips or macaroons. It's far better to start off baking only a dozen or two batches, watching the customer ask questions and taste them, so you can see whether customers actually like them.

You might find your recipe is a winner—or you might find that your customers *really* want chocolate chip cookies, not oatmeal, which you may end up feeding to the trash can. As you will learn along your journey, you can turn that kind of initial misalignment into a learning experience rather than a startup-killing catastrophe. Instead, you will have an opportunity to improve your product, serve your customers better, and build a better and more durable startup.

I'll tell you a story that occurred while I was in the process of writing this book. I have been building my Visionaries platform to help founders get through the minefield of obstacles, some of which my team and I have worked through over the past twenty years. I recall telling my team at one of our startups that I wanted to start demos on Monday. The response was almost the same from all those involved: "OMG, we are not ready!"

I went to the product and engineering team and said, "It's happening."

We started doing demos that Monday and found that the market feedback was already better than anything they had seen, and we were *much* closer to a prototype and even MVP than we thought! I cannot stress this enough. Get the product in front of prospects as soon as you can. Please, in the name of all that is holy, get the product in front of your user advisory board and prospects before *you* even think it's ready. You will thank me for it!

In Phase One (Vision) of the Startup Science Lifecycle, you will put your vision through a validation process, as well as establish there's already a potential market for your product in conjunction with the objectives in creating your North Star. In effect, you've asked the right people (starting with your user advisor board) whether they'd buy a product that delivered a particular kind of value, and they've told you they would.

In Phase Two (Product), the next step is to build out a prototype solution, and a minimum viable product, to show you can deliver the value you've promised. Basically, you've sold people on the idea of your product; now you need to check that your customers still love it when they're *actually experiencing* the minimum viable product. Remember, this isn't the final product, which will be refined with a better design. It does, however, clearly illustrate what the product feels like and how it will work.

It's no exaggeration to say that, once you've successfully found your North Star and your vision, all your energy and resources should go into prototype product development. That means running a lean team, with all your resources going into developing your first products. To put it bluntly, there's no need for sales staff or marketers, or much of anything else, until you have a minimum viable product that's ready to sell, and the first step here is your prototype.

Some advice that I've taken and want to pass along to you is: stop worrying about what can go wrong, and start thinking about what you can learn and what can go right! Remember, what you do today creates tomorrow. To move your product down the field, you must show it to customers. The sooner you do, the sooner you can make progress and get to validation. Once you get validation, your stress level will drop, and your whole team will be invigorated!

Building Out Your Prototype and Minimum Viable Product

Entrepreneurs like me always seem to see problems. Let me ask, how many times do you open a car door, work with a platform, or even use an appliance and say to yourself, "Well, this is a bad design"? If you're like me, it's nonstop. I find large manufacturers miss the most obvious things, and I am always driving my wife crazy saying things like, "Okay, who in the world would do it this way?" The answer is: not a customer. It was more likely an engineer working on the project, who doesn't see it from the consumer's point of view. The point is you cannot validate your own product. You cannot find the flaws. You are too close to it to see what is missing or what needs to be altered. Your customers and users, if (and that's a big if) they feel comfortable, will give you their honest appraisal.

Building out your minimum viable product and prototype team isn't always straightforward, and your hiring decisions will depend on the skills and capabilities the founding team already possesses. If you're chiefly a marketer or a manager, you might need an engineer to help you get your prototype built. If you're first and foremost a coder, you might need a product manager to oversee the user experience (UX) and design aspects required and to ensure the prototype is not overbuilt. It's always in your best interest to make sure the user experience is factored into your product(s).

Pre-Seed Capital

Startups in Phase Two (Product) typically raise their first round of external funding, often colloquially known as pre-seed capital. Such pre-seed capital rounds typically involve investments in the region of $200,000 to $500,000, with current startup valuations of somewhere between $3M and $5M.

Most startups at this phase (Product) do not hire a team. In fact, now there are hundreds of startups designed to help other startups get their prototype built. The advantages are not becoming beholden to the fixed costs associated with a development team and faster iteration cycles, as there are fewer team members to be attached to an idea.

Prototype teams usually come with everything you need and can expand or contract based on your needs and delivery dates. You should attempt to find individuals or companies that focus specifically on working with startups. They are usually more familiar with limited budgets and tight timelines. Your prototype team, wherever you find them, should be biased toward progress, not perfection. I highly recommend this approach when you are this early in the lifecycle.

Beyond the raw skills needed to produce and hone a prototype, you'll also need someone to own the process of product development. That's subtly different from simply building the prototype product. Your product manager doesn't necessarily need to be able to create new products with their own two hands, but they *do* need to be able to understand and advocate for your customers and users and to ensure the prototype team ultimately comes up with a product that is well aligned with your customers' needs, wants, and pain points.

The product manager is "the voice of the customer and user," and their primary mission is, in a sense, to translate the insights first encountered during your vision validation process into the nuts and bolts of a prototype product. Their first task during this phase (Product) is to gather prototype feedback from potential customers, user advisory board members, and industry advisory board members. They must then immediately attempt to harness those insights to advocate for the needs of your ideal customer and persona as you work to build your prototype product, and ultimately minimum viable product. Product managers are typically engaging with both ideal industry board members and user advisory board members on a weekly or biweekly basis during this phase. Timely, insightful feedback is critical to a successful Phase Two (Product).

During these conversations, the product manager is creating what are most commonly known as "product requirements," which are a compilation of user/customer stories. User/customer stories reflect the many pieces of product feedback and research you have obtained, and describe what the product should achieve for a given type of user. For example, "I work for the [ideal customer profile]. I want [this] so that I can do [that]."

As you build your prototype and conduct research, the number of user/customer stories and product requirements you create will explode.

Don't worry, you don't need to act on them all at once, but you will want to prioritize and track them in some type of project management system. Your product requirements and user/customer stories will break into two buckets—current priorities slated for development, which are a list of items you build with your team in prioritized order, and backlog items, which you do want to work on, but don't want to prioritize at this current moment.

While your product production schedule might vary depending on the product you are building, you should ideally be testing a new version of your prototype every two to three weeks with your users. Less time won't allow your prototype team to make any substantial progress. More time will likely allow "feature creep" to seep in. (Which means having excessive features creep into your product progress. These are features that make the product too complex to use or too expensive to buy.) This will delay your company's overall lifecycle progress.

As your product team progresses, they will also maintain, as the voice of the customer, comprehensive ideal customer profiles (ICPs). These are documents or presentations that contain all the information you have on how to best represent your customers to internal teams. But ICPs are not just about storing the information. Creating ICPs also means making it clear how each decision will impact or be perceived by customers and users. Then such insights will be translated into action items that Engineering can implement, Marketing can build a narrative around, and Sales can tell the right story.

Steve Jobs said, "Customers don't know what they want until they see it." I hear this often. It's true—they do have cognitive biases that may prevent them from realizing the ideal solution, but they do understand their problems and whether your solution solves them. When you show a customer and user the problem and they agree, *boom*! Building your prototype will ultimately require many versions of user/customer stories and proposed solutions. As a result, a prototype is not completed in a single iteration.

The Power of Customer Advocacy in Validating Your Product Prototype

To understand the power of an effective product prototype, look at two electric cars: the Nissan Leaf and the Tesla Model 3. Both sprang from the same basic vision: a capable, technologically advanced electric vehicle with mass-market appeal. But the end products are very different, and those differences are grounded in the two automakers' understandings of who the customer is, and what they really want. Like or dislike Tesla, they certainly build an amazing electric car.

In contrast to Tesla, there's nothing *wrong* with the Leaf per se—it moves when you step on the accelerator, it's affordable, eco-friendly, and it ticks a whole bunch of other important boxes. If you'd gone to consumers or dealerships and told them all that as part of your vision validation, they'd certainly have told you there would be real demand for your product. But if you dig deeper by asking the right questions, in the right way, to the right people (such as advisory boards), you might have discovered that there are many jokes making fun of Leaf drivers moving at the speed of a snail going uphill in a January snowstorm or struggling to merge onto a highway without holding back traffic.

What does that say? While there is certainly a market for an affordable, eco-friendly car, a Tesla is reaching out to a higher-end customer who wants more and is willing to pay for it. For example, it must be fast—and not just fast, but exciting. It must lift your spirits and make you come alive. If you have ever driven a Tesla, it most certainly does that. This is why selecting the most representative and diverse pool of members for your industry advisory and user advisory boards is so important. You need to ensure you understand the root causes and beliefs of your prospects.

That's where Tesla excelled, of course. Their product managers understood the need to build a car that moves fast, gets your pulse racing, and makes you feel like a visitor from the future. Thanks to Tesla's product managers and their understanding of *their* ideal customer profile, the startup's engineers didn't just set out to build another electric car; they set out to build an experience. Because they understood their customers on an emotional level, they were able to build a product that truly catered to their needs—one they'd get excited about. I have made this mistake myself a few times, so pay close attention to the customer and user/customer stories to make sure you are not just listening, but *hearing*, the feedback. As Simon Sinek says, "There is a difference between listening and waiting for your turn to talk."

Minimum Viable Product–Proof of Customer and Product-Market Fit

When I started an applied environmental biotech startup, Vision Environmental Solutions, I was standing over a disgusting wastewater pit near the grease trap, trying to figure out what form the product should take. The problem was clear; the product was not. I'd only popped in to talk with a friend who'd opened the restaurant. He happened to be outside trying to deal with the problem and couldn't do our planned lunch. The disgusting wastewater pit near the grease trap was a problem that both founders and investors had anxiety over. It was one of those big thorny problems that needed a solution, which, when found and proven effective, becomes the beginning of a highly successful startup. Now I just needed to figure out the right way to solve it.

While my friend saw a messy, smelly water pit, with an expensive recurring monthly charge that did not solve the problem but masked it, I saw something different. I saw that part of the problem came from the companies that supposedly solved the "smelly water issue." These companies were run by industry veterans who'd spent years, or decades, doing things the same way, because this was simply "how it was always done," and was how they made a living (perfect example of a persona issue).

Instead of finding innovative solutions, they used procedures that temporarily masked or solved the immediate problem. Even mentioning that there could be other options to these companies caused the same kind of reaction the oil interests and auto companies had when Tesla announced their first electric car. Let's just say it was not welcoming.

The incumbents in the space did not understand that their business would not disappear if they evolved and innovated solutions for the disgusting water that could be more efficient and more profitable. Customers weren't sure how to connect the dots and turn that problem into a product, but they would leave their existing solution providers as soon as another solution became available.

My friend was used to using solutions that did not check all the boxes. The biggest, in this case, was the recurring monthly cleaning procedure that was expensive, messy, and smelly. When I started the research on the ecosystem to "get smart," I quite literally was elbow deep. After several weeks, I introduced the solution, with the help of my friend who owned the restaurant. It received initial validation . . . it worked and solved the problem. I had validated the vision, so when I reached out to potential customers, they asked if they could see for themselves. I arrived with my prototype, a five-gallon bucket of freeze-dried bacteria, and poured it into the system. I told them that I would be back the following day to see how it worked. The next day, the system was clearly better and, within a few days, completely clear. Validated!

Next, I created a brand, alongside a better delivery method, all based on the feedback I received from customers. My brand pitch focused on the customer doing the work, but, as I would soon find out, customers (the restaurant owners and managers) did not want to do the work, no matter how much money they saved. By giving my customers my brand pitch, I was able to realize a very important thing. I could not validate the minimum viable product (MVP) as it stood. Knowing this allowed me the opportunity to tap the brakes on product development and do some self-reflection. I realized the product was not just a product, but a product-enabled service, meaning the product would need to come with someone to provide the service.

This situation occurred because, while my MVP did the job, it did not solve the root problem, because I had not defined the problem completely in the first place. The solution was something much simpler: a passive hydrocarbon solution from a truck pumping away in their parking lot. Price was not the issue, as customers never wanted to even come near the problem. More specifically, the customer story was "I am a restaurant manager. I work at a successful restaurant. I want to dispose of hydrocarbons without smell or disruption to my customers, so that I don't scare off customers." The problem was clear. The part that was not included was the cost or the fact that he wanted to solve the problem but not get involved. In other words, he didn't want to "get his hands dirty" . . . literally.

My initial startup product counted on a DIY approach and cost savings. If I had continued with that approach, I would have spent all my seed money rolling out a go-to-market (GTM) strategy without properly understanding the entire problem set.

I went back and tried to sell my product to the people who were already pumping grease out of manholes and asked them to add pouring the product into the manholes. This didn't work for various reasons, so I went to the source to find out who was responsible for the pumpers. This was the local municipalities. They became my customers, buying the product and including it in the routine tasks of the pumpers. We had handled the problem at its source. This process drastically changed my MVP in the startup. However, without the iterative product prototype process, I'm confident that this startup would have failed entirely. This is why it's important to be flexible, or agile, especially when it comes to successfully knowing your customers and selling your product.

As you can see, doing this kind of prototype testing allows you to reframe failure into a learning opportunity. When my first product and approach fell short, I didn't simply give up and go home. I took those lessons and responded as I learned. Along the way, I gathered important win and loss data from customers—real-world data that helped me improve and prove the final iteration, which really had what it took to go the distance. The final piece was simply to add a service technician to deposit the product for the restaurants. I had finally created a product-enabled service that solved the problem end-to-end . . . and no one owning or working in the restaurant had to get their hands dirty.

This story brings us to the real litmus test for your MVP: finding your first customer. That doesn't necessarily mean your first *paying* customer, but it does mean finding someone—or, ideally, several someones—who will use your product in the real world and get real value from it. Think about it like this—when a chef wants to open a new eatery, they don't just throw the doors open and fire up the ovens. Instead, they do a soft open, with a carefully selected group of local bigwigs and influencers invited to eat for free. That gives the chef a chance to tweak the menu and to prove that people actually want to eat in their restaurant. This is effectively your user/customer advisory board—those that you invite to your beta and who work with you to create a product so attractive that they pay for it, and in the end, become your first customers. The ultimate validation is when your user advisory board becomes paying customers. So choose your user advisory board right, or your validation will be flawed. Your ideal customer profile and personas must be correct, as you can see here.

Product validation is often like that: if you can show your investors a bunch of licked-clean plates and customer feedback cards showing that your menu is market-ready, they'll be far more likely to give you the funds you need. And those clean plates and review cards really matter, because product validation is about proving your MVP to yourself and, of course, investors. Next, it's important to think about how you'll communicate the results of the process.

Once you have completed your prototype, as well as your MVP, you'll be ready to move to Phase Three (Go-to-Market) in the Startup Science Lifecycle. You'll have spent time gathering feedback on your MVP from your industry advisory board and user advisory board and will have already begun to make changes based on that feedback. You're also likely in a position to raise your seed round and begin to execute on your vision. It is likely that it has been six to eighteen months since you completed Phase One (Vision).

CHAPTER WRAP-UP

At this point, you are continuing to improve your product as your startup scales. Your scaling-specific KPI is linked to leading indicators. You are growing at a rate that is somewhere between comfortable and uncomfortable.

You're also likely in a position to raise your series seed round, if needed. It's likely been six to twelve months. If, and only if, you can confidently answer yes to completing all of the above are you ready to move on to Phase Three (Go-to-Market). The goal of the next section is to leverage all that you have learned up to this point to develop your go-to-market strategy.

You now have your prototype and MVP. You have launched two critical functional areas in your business—Shared Services and Product. With your internal operations established, it is now time to shift your focus and resources (people, money, time) to the growth side of the business to get your product in the hands of your customers.

CHAPTER EIGHT

Phase Three: Go-to-Market for Startups

> Marketing is no longer about the stuff that you make, but about the stories you tell.
>
> **—Seth Godin, American author, former dotcom startup executive**

In 2023, my quest was to do a monthlong water fast for my overall health. However, this was not as simple as not eating. The clinic I visited offered a program that included a process of "pre-feeding," which started by eating only raw food, vegetables, and fruit, then shifted to vegetables and vegetable juices, then water. All of which was done based on my blood tests, body vitals, the way I felt, and my energy levels. I did not just dive in.

The go-to-market phase (GTM) is also a process, *not* something you just dive into. What I mean is that you start with a crawl-walk-run playbook. It includes testing, metrics, and yes, your instincts. But your instincts are enhanced by real factual data points. And like the fast, every step is monitored, and only when it's safe do you progress. Your GTM should have a plan just as my fast had a plan, with steps and checkpoints that include more than just sales and marketing. Like a fast, it's more than just not eating. Your whole body is affected. Likewise, your GTM affects the whole business, meaning you have to plan holistically.

Today, when I ask founders the very, very important question "What is your go-to-market (GTM) plan?" I am blown away by the answers. Almost never do I see an inclusive GTM plan. I see advertising strategies, sales strategies, marketing strategies. Those are things that happen during your GTM, sure, but a GTM is a plan made up of parts and strategies for the other functional areas that will unquestionably play a role in the success of the customer acquisition and retention efforts.

In reality, a startup only enters, or "goes to market," one time in the maturity of their lifecycle. After the initial launch and entry to the market (successful or unsuccessful), your startup is considered "in-market."

In life, we have been warned about the importance of making a good first impression and how hard it is to influence someone who has already made an opinion or passed judgment. Business is no different. Think back to a time you spent money on something that didn't work or failed to meet the expectations set by the marketing that sold it—how do you feel about that company or brand today? Would you be willing to recommend it to others? How much money have you spent with them since that experience?

Unfortunately, misguided investor expectations around "revenue" have forced many companies to prematurely enter the market, taking on valuable customers that fit the ICP, with a product that does not yet meet their expectations or has clunky internal operations that create a negative user experience. These are two of the most common reasons for failure among startups in this phase (Go-to-Market).

Series Seed Round

Startups in Phase Three typically raise their third round of external funding, often colloquially known as "series seed round." These rounds typically involve investments in the region of $500,000 to $5M, with current startup valuations of somewhere between $6M and $15M.

Not only are efficient internal operations critical for customer acquisition and retention in the GTM phase, but they will also be a leading indicator of your ability to raise capital and eventually exit your business, as due diligence is typically required before and after a capital raise.

What Is a Go-to-Market Strategy?

What does go-to-market (GTM) mean? This term has been widely used and abused across industries for many years. Still, there is no universal definition. In my opinion, that is because your GTM depends on where your startup is in the Startup Science Lifecycle.

In large enterprise startups, GTM is reserved primarily for the Sales and Marketing functional areas. Typically, it represents a new brand message, or a new product offering, and is intended to make a big splash in a crowded market, where it will desperately try to get the attention of potential buyers.

To provide a more precise definition for GTM that applies to *startups*, you have to look across every functional area of your startup. This is because, in established businesses, they have built out functional areas, so adding a new product is part of ongoing operations. In a startup, it's the first time you are introducing your new product. I have seen startups that are so successful they disappointed customers (think Tesla, a company that sold far more cars than they had manufactured, which resulted in long customer waiting times for their automobiles), and those who get it wrong and fail completely (think Segway).

Here is how I define it within my own ecosystem of startups: GTM for a *startup* includes a strategic understanding of your ideal customer profile (ICP) and persona's journey, which includes when, where, why, and how they buy, combined with effectively paired marketing assets, like narrative and content strategy. Because your startup is not a solo sport, you must make sure all functional areas are aligned and ready. The process starts in Marketing, moves to Sales, then to Service, and all the time affecting Shared Services and, of course, Product and Engineering. With a basic definition now in place, let's move on.

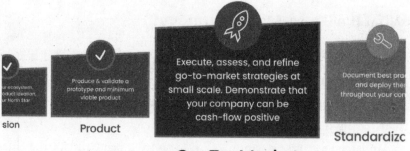

Go-To-Market

Phase Three (Go-to-Market) is the last major hurdle you will have to overcome before starting to really accelerate your growth. Once you have a product, a customer, and a solid GTM strategy, you'll be ready to raise your series seed round and start putting the machinery in place to sell your products. Stories of startups being unprepared can be found everywhere; they show up in the truth under the data where you find the wrong team or product-market fit. The real story requires some digging, but you learn things like the team was unprepared for the customers, there were pricing issues, and more. GTM preparation is no different than anything you do as a startup founder. Prepare for what you know, prepare for what you don't know, and expect change . . . lots of it!

What Qualifies as Go-to-Market?

As I briefly mentioned in the last chapter, your GTM will consist of a couple of key components—some strategic and some tactical. While your GTM will change as you progress through the lifecycle, the core components and feedback improvement loop are *always* the same.

Every GTM starts with the creation of your product narratives, which describe your product as it relates to your prospects, and your content marketing strategy, which describes the pieces of content you create, and where they will be syndicated to generate demand.

Next, you'll define your pipeline management strategy, which are the precise steps you'll follow to manage the customer demand that you've previously generated, toward an ultimate sale of your product.

Now that you've tackled the marketing and sales components of your GTM, you'll also ensure that every other functional area is prepared to support your GTM including Product, Engineering, and Shared Services (such as IT, HR, Finance, and Legal). This is the most commonly missed component, which can easily torpedo even the most well-planned GTM.

Finally, you'll close the loop by implementing an agile process to capture feedback so you can refine your GTM strategy to ensure you're always improving your ability to generate demand and convert prospects.

As you prepare for your initial GTM, there are lots of areas beyond sales and marketing that you need to be prepared to support (IT, HR, Finance, and Legal). Stay agile and be prepared to gather and act on feedback quickly.

Go-to-Market—Demand

Let's start out talking about the customer's journey with a journey of my own. One year, I decided to learn bullfighting for a number of not very good reasons. Before you get a vision of me dancing around an arena with a two-ton bull, you should understand that I was what is called a *novillero torero* (junior bullfighter). Novillero toreros typically start by fighting younger bulls to reduce the risk of getting hurt. This endeavor required research, not unlike what anyone does when they are trying to learn a new subject. I started in a search engine, typing keywords, until I caught on and started following a trail. I was able to read articles, listen to podcasts, and watch videos. The point is, once I was in that process, everything with which I engaged was demand content around bullfighting. This is called the "customer journey," and it is led by a narrative spine and content strategy.

The customer journey is a flow chart that follows your customer's avatar. When I talk to founders, I say, "Let's suppose you want to sell a marketing software product. The obvious first step is knowing to whom you will be selling, followed closely by figuring out how to get in front of them in the normal course of their work life."

If I were in marketing, I would be looking up keywords like "demand generation," "content marketing," and so on. Like many new adventures today, the first step in the journey is to search. But where? Well, it depends on how I want to consume the information. Do I like to watch videos? Do I listen to podcasts? Do I read articles? When I do these things, where do I go? YouTube? Publications like *Forbes* or *Wired*? As you do this, think of mapping it out on a flow chart. The chart will show you the cross sections of engagement and align your narrative and your content . . . then *boom*, you're on the organic path!

The formula for a narrative spine is simple, but it is a creative process that requires a massive lift of content creation and syndication. It requires any founder and/or business owner to spend time developing it.

It starts with your content marketing strategy. Utilizing your North Star and ecosystem to create narratives, you will guide all your content marketing and messaging. (I told you we're going to use the North Star and ecosystem everywhere.) These narratives will be used for your content marketing strategy, which always starts with the core types of content:

- Watch (YouTube, TikTok, Instagram)
- Listen (podcasts or webinars)
- Read (LinkedIn articles, blogs)
- Experience (demos, free trials).

Over time you can add additional types, including infographics, influencers, streaming ads, explainer videos, and more, to match additional marketing channels that you activate. Once you've built your initial product narratives and formed your content marketing strategy, you're ready to start activating your awareness campaign, which can also serve as a lead generation machine.

Generating Demand

Now that you've got your basic GTM foundation in place, let's put it to use to generate demand for your product. By creating meaningful, engaging, and targeted content that fits your narrative and talks to your ideal customer profile, you attract prospects rather than seeking them out. It is the difference between push (cold calling) and pull (content) marketing. Unlike cold-calling customers, demand generation:

- Reduces overall customer acquisition costs.
- Does not disrupt your prospects' day.

Creating a Narrative Spine and Content Strategy

In the old days, we would sit down and dial for dollars. Cold calling was king. But cold calling is incredibly expensive and very much out of favor these days.

Cold calling has become a terrible model for attracting customers, and here's why: before a salesperson calls, they need to understand who they are talking to (ICP/persona).

When a cold caller calls one of your prospects, they are doing three things:

1. Verifying the contact data of that prospect
2. Introducing your business
3. Warming up the prospect to potentially engaging with your business

The first problem is the unpredictable "hit rate" of even reaching your prospect by phone. Next, the setup of the follow-up call is pure pain. Cold calling is simply a flawed system, because it relies on enticing a person without having any context as to who they are calling and what that person's wants and needs are. In short, it's a disruption, and the individual receiving the phone call knows nothing about what your business sells and whether or not they have any interest. In short, cold calling is known as "push" marketing (also defined today as "pushy" marketing). You are trying to push the customer to your message.

Demand generation (DG) flips this on its head. It is a completely different animal altogether. Nowadays, everyone is using the Internet to learn, get news, and communicate ideas. Demand generation provides customers with what they are looking for with meaningful, solid content at the time, and in the manner the customer wants to consume it. It is effectively verifying the contact, introducing the business, and warming up the prospect without the issues you face with cold calls. If done correctly, this method is, without question, the powerhouse strategy startups should focus on during their GTM phase. Demand generation requires carefully crafted, meaningful content to be available to potential customers in order to pull them toward your product or service. "Pull" marketing, as it has been termed, will cost less, but it will require military-like precision and focus, so don't cut corners on the content. Produce meaningful content that your ICP/persona cares about, and it will pay for itself! Do it wrong, and you will destroy your brand.

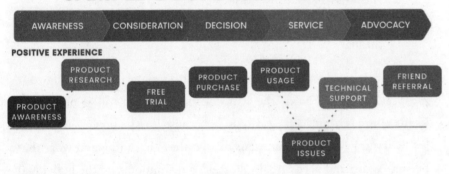

SAMPLE CUSTOMER JOURNEY

It All Begins with a Narrative Spine

A narrative is a sequenced, topical theme that guides your customer-facing messaging and content production. Think of the narrative spine as the spine of your business, and each vertebra as a subject. Each subject has individual topics, which are the content you will create. Your narrative spine tells you what to focus the content on. It also allows you to create cohesive messaging across activities, which reinforces messaging for the potential customer, and to reuse content across activities.

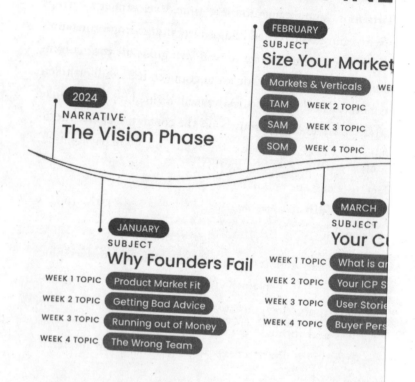

To master the narrative spine, review your North Star and customer research to create a list of subjects based on the needs, and wants of your ICP. Then, underneath each subject, specific topics.

Narrative Spine for Electric Car Customers	
Subject: The Cost of Fuel	**Subject:** The Carbon Foss Produces
Topic: Electric cars cost 0.02 cents of the cost of fossil fuel.	**Topic:** Electric cars emit ze bon from the tailpipe.

- Reduces sales costs by automating everything up to the point that the prospect shows interest.

Generally, you and your team should decide on a six- to twelve-month plan to test your product narratives and content strategy, with a review and subsequent adjustments every three months. The goal is to test with a variety of DG methods, measure what works, and focus on tactics that deliver results.

Now, let's walk through how to build your product narratives, select your content marketing activities, determine your KPIs, and ensure Sales, Marketing, and Customer Service work together.

Choosing Your Narratives

Does your ideal customer profile (ICP) identify with specific messaging and stories? This is the question you want to focus on as you create your narrative. Once again, we look at the end result we are seeking when we start the process.

The goal of your narrative is to align all your content marketing around a specific topic that your ICP responds to favorably. Marketing activities (at least your content-centric ones) will align to that narrative each month.

The messaging you tested with advisors during the prototype, and the work done in Phase One (Vision), are the basis for your narratives. If the narratives are not self-evident, go back to Phase One and work on your North Star statements.

Potential narratives also show up in the product user/customer stories. For example, if you've completed your North Star user stories (detailed earlier), you'll have statements like "As a founder, I would like to avoid failure by understanding why 90 percent of startups fail and, instead, learn to succeed." You can see potential narratives in the phrases "avoid failure" and "learn to succeed."

Select six high-level storylines to test over the next six months to see what your customers respond to most favorably. Using this book as an example:

January = Why StartupScience.io Can Help Founders

February = Explaining the Startup Science Lifecycle

March = North Star, etc.

And so on . . .

Put them in an order that makes sense, prioritizing based on expected responsiveness. Logical progress can be used to prioritize, but don't expect that a customer will recognize the sequence of your narratives. They aren't paying that close attention to what you are doing from month to month, so make sure each storyline stands on its own. In other words, don't make one month's storyline contingent on them having seen, heard, or read the previous month's storyline.

Every three months, host a quarterly meeting to review results and adjust the narratives based on data you'll collect during demand-generation activities.

It's important to keep everyone at your startup up to date on narratives, from both an awareness and a cross-functional task alignment perspective.

Picking Your Content Narrative Topics

There are standard content activities, and some that will be unique opportunities based on your ecosystem. But remember that all activities have the same goal of driving potential customers to engage with you. Marketing's job is to reach potential customers, determine if they are likely to purchase, and hand off a warm lead to your sales team at the right time.

Content activities can be viewed by how the user accesses the content, through reading, listening, watching, or experiencing. Always keep in mind that not everyone has the same preference or ability to digest content activities in the same way. So, you want to use a mix of methods to attract and appeal to all of your potential customers.

NOTE: In Phase One (Vision), you listed out a bunch of these "watering holes" for your ideal customer profile. You may have learned through interviews with your user advisory board the types of content they prefer. These are used to create your list of content activities.

Here are some examples of content activities:

- Blog posts on your site or another company's site
- Articles placed on your site and in industry publications (on- or offline)
- Webinars and other online events
- Podcasts (being a guest on others' and/or through your own)
- Emails to your database or co-marketing with databases from other businesses

When you move to measuring success and iterating on what future expectations are, you'll set "plan" numbers against each activity. For example:

- Blog (ours)—two posts per month
- Guest Blog—one post per month

You will want to make a schedule of posts or any ongoing marketing you are planning to do.

Pick Measurable Key Performance Indicators

In Phase Five (Optimization), key performance indicators (KPIs) are covered in depth, because marketing and sales activities must be measurable. We've all made the mistake of setting KPIs that we simply can't measure. If you do so, you'll be unable to determine whether your product narratives and/or content marketing are working. I mention this now to make you aware, as you work through the marketing process, that you will need to use measurable KPIs for all marketing activities. So, for each marketing activity, you want to ensure you've recorded a response when it occurs (example, clicks through to the blog posts).

If a prospect in your ideal customer profile reads one piece of your content and another prospect reads ten pieces of your content, which prospect is more likely to buy from you? As you may have guessed, the second prospect, since they have demonstrated an affinity for your narratives.

The goal is to have a potential customer engage with your content. To read or listen, watch or experience, and then to demonstrate interest through continued engagement, which creates another measure for us called "propensity to buy" (PTB). This means, if the prospect has a high PTB, they are more likely to buy from you.

This is also known as lead scoring. We need a scoreboard that indicates who has digested what content and how much of it they've consumed. For simplicity (because this is getting complicated), let's give a score of 1 for each blog or podcast engaged by the prospect. If Rita from Acme Corp (a prospect in your ideal customer profile) engages with three pieces of content, we might decide that is enough for Sales to make contact.

GTM is always (not just in the very beginning of the lifecycle) composed of three steps: plan, execute, and iterate. All three steps are critical.

All right! Now you have your product narratives (iterated every three months), and you have specific content marketing activities that you will test each month (plan, actual, difference). As prospects engage, you are building up an individual "score" for them. In essence, you will see which prospects engage the most and are your best bet to reach out to.

Proof That Demand Generation Is Working

According to Dr. Stephen R. Covey, all things are created twice—first in the mind and then in the real world. Physical creations follow mental ones, like homes built according to blueprints. To make your deepest desires a reality, you first need to see and understand what those desires are. So, in short, as we have discussed all throughout this book, beginning with the end in mind is so important. You want to visualize your life, career, or a specific project in the way you want it to turn out before you actually begin pursuing it. The question I get asked more than anything is, "How? How is it possible that you do all these things?" Well, this is how! When you make this conscious effort, you take much greater control over your circumstances or, in this case, your buyers.

Your foundational GTM strategy leads to scored engagement with your content, website, or product from prospective buyers. When the prospect has engaged with enough content, meeting a predetermined score threshold that your teams will decide upon in advance, the software will drop the prospective buyer into your relationship management software and—*boom*! Your lead generation machine is up and running. This warm lead is now familiar with your startup and product(s) and has shown a level of interest that alerts your teams, and primes both the sales representative and lead for a successful sales pipeline process. I call this exercise the "mindset shift." With even more advanced programs, there's endless room to nerd out and refine data points from conversation rates to content engagement percentages; getting into the weeds of a successful customer journey to find opportunities for further insight or streamlining can be very exciting!

Mindset Shift

Everyone has a mindset, and sometimes it needs to shift. When I did one of my annual quests, I faced this head-on. At the time, I was looking out over a two-thousand-foot drop with a parachute in my hand, getting ready to BASE jump off a cliff. Since my mind has always been my greatest challenge, I've come to understand the power of the mind.

Your mind can be shifted in many directions. This is often the case with customers who have a mindset and, like me, do not want to be pushed into buying something . . . or, in this case, off a cliff. You can't push your prospects. Push sales have proven repeatedly that such a strategy doesn't work, and in the odd chance they do, the data says that those prospects have a ten times greater chance of churn. (Customer "churn" is the percentage of customers that stop using your company's product or service during a certain time frame. You can calculate churn rate by dividing the number of customers you lost during that time period—say a quarter—by the number of customers you had at the beginning of that time period.)

The reality is that you can spend ten times more money trying to create mindset shifts over ten Zoom calls, or you can pull customers to you by providing meaningful content focused on your target persona. By letting quality content do the work of the ten Zoom calls, the customer is making their own decision, rather than being pushed. Using the natural path of least resistance and providing them with value will most often drive them to you. In other words, they change their mindset and want to buy what you are selling. When I BASE jumped, I used the landscape and the moment of energy to shift my mindset. I then jumped when I was ready by first getting my mind shift and then being proactive. Like Stephen Covey says, "There's a mental, or first creation, and a physical or second creation to all things." And as I've learned, people don't like having someone else push them to create a mindset shift.

In order to make a mindset shift in our buyers, particularly those who are already set in their ways of doing (or buying) something, we need to try to shift their way of thinking. For example, if you're an iPhone customer and we're trying to sell you an Android, it will require a mindset shift. To do this effectively, you need to understand where they are currently (and why) and where we would like to take them (and why). It's the old "current state" versus "desired future state" scenario. By embracing the principle of beginning with the end in mind, we can answer two questions to develop a high-converting campaign:

- What does a buyer need to *learn* in order to feel pride at the end of their journey?
- What does a buyer need to *see* in order to make a mindset shift?

Answers to these can be as simple as creating a formula for *teaching* the buyer about the return on investment (ROI) associated with purchasing your product or service, then *showing* ROI evidence in a similar business or providing them with customer references that highlight success.

To create an individual propensity to buy score, the prospect has to be present in your customer relationship management (CRM) software. This happens either by manually entering that person (name, business, and email address) or by them "registering" with you for additional content. If a lead or prospect asks for a call, then call them! If they don't, then you will ask them for a call when the score tells you they are ready. By repeatedly testing and assessing your scoring rubric and conversion rates, you'll be able to home in on the right score threshold for your startup.

For example, let's pick a score of 3, based upon the number of engagements with your content. Once a lead has engaged with three pieces of content from you, crossing that predetermined threshold, they are designated as a marketing qualified lead (MQL). This means that, based upon your tested marketing strategy, they are qualified to move to the sales lead assessment process.

MQL Scoring Threshold

The lead is then passed to Sales (usually through a CRM process). Sales will re-qualify the lead:

- Do they want to engage with sales representatives?
- Do they align with your ideal customer profile (ICP)?
- Do they have a real need that can be solved by your product?

If Sales accepts the lead from Marketing, we call this a sales-qualified lead (SQL). This is important, because it confirms that your marketing strategy and team are functioning properly and delivered a qualified lead to your sales representatives. This is a *huge* step in your success!

Once Sales takes the lead, it will enter the sales pipeline, where sales pipeline management will take the baton to handle the SQL.

Sales Process and Management

Sales pipeline management strategy is primarily focused on moving prospects through the different phases, from SQL to purchase. You'll typically have fields associated with each phase, including type, status, contract value, probability, and estimated close date, which come together to provide you with a weighted pipeline value. Before we get to the specifics that you'll use to assemble your strategy, let's review a few of the general principles:

1. Every lead transfer from Marketing to Sales must be through a measurable action in the CRM (like a conversion from lead to prospect or transfer of an account). It should not be done manually.
2. Once a lead reaches Sales, it immediately becomes part of the sales pipeline with a predefined pipeline phase.
3. Each pipeline phase in the CRM must have defined entry/exit criteria and required sales actions. These should be recorded and socialized across your organization.

Creating a Narrative Spine and Content Strategy

In the old days, we would sit down and dial for dollars. Cold calling was king. But cold calling is incredibly expensive and very much out of favor these days.

Cold calling has become a terrible model for attracting customers, and here's why: before a salesperson calls, they need to understand who they are talking to (ICP/persona).

When a cold caller calls one of your prospects, they are doing three things:

1. Verifying the contact data of that prospect
2. Introducing your business
3. Warming up the prospect to potentially engaging with your business

The first problem is the unpredictable "hit rate" of even reaching your prospect by phone. Next, the setup of the follow-up call is pure pain. Cold calling is simply a flawed system, because it relies on enticing a person without having any context as to who they are calling and what that person's wants and needs are. In short, it's a disruption, and the individual receiving the phone call knows nothing about what your business sells and whether or not they have any interest. In short, cold calling is known as "push" marketing (also defined today as "pushy" marketing). You are trying to push the customer to your message.

Demand generation (DG) flips this on its head. It is a completely different animal altogether. Nowadays, everyone is using the Internet to learn, get news, and communicate ideas. Demand generation provides customers with what they are looking for with meaningful, solid content at the time, and in the manner the customer wants to consume it. It is effectively verifying the contact, introducing the business, and warming up the prospect without the issues you face with cold calls. If done correctly, this method is, without question, the powerhouse strategy startups should focus on during their GTM phase. Demand generation requires carefully crafted, meaningful content to be available to potential customers in order to pull them toward your product or service. "Pull" marketing, as it has been termed, will cost less, but it will require military-like precision and focus, so don't cut corners on the content. Produce meaningful content that your ICP/persona cares about, and it will pay for itself! Do it wrong, and you will destroy your brand.

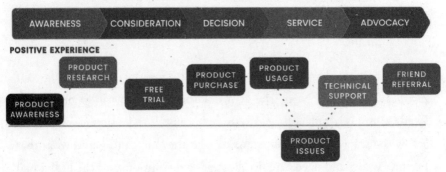

It All Begins with a Narrative Spine

A narrative is a sequenced, topical theme that guides your customer-facing messaging and content production. Think of the narrative spine as the spine of your business, and each vertebra as a subject. Each subject has individual topics, which are the content you will create. Your narrative spine tells you what to focus the content on. It also allows you to create cohesive messaging across activities, which reinforces messaging for the potential customer, and to reuse content across activities.

NARRATIVE SPINE

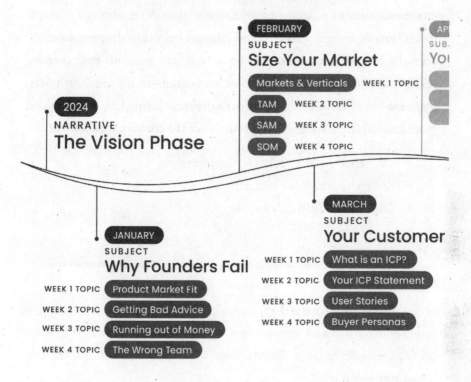

To master the narrative spine, review your North Star and do your customer research to create a list of subjects based on the interests, needs, and wants of your ICP. Then, underneath each subject, list more specific topics.

Narrative Spine for Electric Car Customers	
Subject: The Cost of Fuel	**Subject:** The Carbon Fossil Fuel Produces
Topic: Electric cars cost 0.02 cents of the cost of fossil fuel.	**Topic:** Electric cars emit zero carbon from the tailpipe.

The formula for a narrative spine is simple, but it is a creative process that requires a massive lift of content creation and syndication. It requires any founder and/or business owner to spend time developing it.

It starts with your content marketing strategy. Utilizing your North Star and ecosystem to create narratives, you will guide all your content marketing and messaging. (I told you we're going to use the North Star and ecosystem everywhere.) These narratives will be used for your content marketing strategy, which always starts with the core types of content:

- Watch (YouTube, TikTok, Instagram)
- Listen (podcasts or webinars)
- Read (LinkedIn articles, blogs)
- Experience (demos, free trials).

Over time you can add additional types, including infographics, influencers, streaming ads, explainer videos, and more, to match additional marketing channels that you activate. Once you've built your initial product narratives and formed your content marketing strategy, you're ready to start activating your awareness campaign, which can also serve as a lead generation machine.

Generating Demand

Now that you've got your basic GTM foundation in place, let's put it to use to generate demand for your product. By creating meaningful, engaging, and targeted content that fits your narrative and talks to your ideal customer profile, you attract prospects rather than seeking them out. It is the difference between push (cold calling) and pull (content) marketing. Unlike cold-calling customers, demand generation:

- Reduces overall customer acquisition costs.
- Does not disrupt your prospects' day.

- Reduces sales costs by automating everything up to the point that the prospect shows interest.

Generally, you and your team should decide on a six- to twelve-month plan to test your product narratives and content strategy, with a review and subsequent adjustments every three months. The goal is to test with a variety of DG methods, measure what works, and focus on tactics that deliver results.

Now, let's walk through how to build your product narratives, select your content marketing activities, determine your KPIs, and ensure Sales, Marketing, and Customer Service work together.

Choosing Your Narratives

Does your ideal customer profile (ICP) identify with specific messaging and stories? This is the question you want to focus on as you create your narrative. Once again, we look at the end result we are seeking when we start the process.

The goal of your narrative is to align all your content marketing around a specific topic that your ICP responds to favorably. Marketing activities (at least your content-centric ones) will align to that narrative each month.

The messaging you tested with advisors during the prototype, and the work done in Phase One (Vision), are the basis for your narratives. If the narratives are not self-evident, go back to Phase One and work on your North Star statements.

Potential narratives also show up in the product user/customer stories. For example, if you've completed your North Star user stories (detailed earlier), you'll have statements like "As a founder, I would like to avoid failure by understanding why 90 percent of startups fail and, instead, learn to succeed." You can see potential narratives in the phrases "avoid failure" and "learn to succeed."

Select six high-level storylines to test over the next six months to see what your customers respond to most favorably. Using this book as an example:

January = Why StartupScience.io Can Help Founders

February = Explaining the Startup Science Lifecycle

March = North Star, etc.

And so on . . .

Put them in an order that makes sense, prioritizing based on expected responsiveness. Logical progress can be used to prioritize, but don't expect that a customer will recognize the sequence of your narratives. They aren't paying that close attention to what you are doing from month to month, so make sure each storyline stands on its own. In other words, don't make one month's storyline contingent on them having seen, heard, or read the previous month's storyline.

Every three months, host a quarterly meeting to review results and adjust the narratives based on data you'll collect during demand-generation activities.

It's important to keep everyone at your startup up to date on narratives, from both an awareness and a cross-functional task alignment perspective.

Picking Your Content Narrative Topics

There are standard content activities, and some that will be unique opportunities based on your ecosystem. But remember that all activities have the same goal of driving potential customers to engage with you. Marketing's job is to reach potential customers, determine if they are likely to purchase, and hand off a warm lead to your sales team at the right time.

Content activities can be viewed by how the user accesses the content, through reading, listening, watching, or experiencing. Always keep in mind that not everyone has the same preference or ability to digest content activities in the same way. So, you want to use a mix of methods to attract and appeal to all of your potential customers.

NOTE: In Phase One (Vision), you listed out a bunch of these "watering holes" for your ideal customer profile. You may have learned through interviews with your user advisory board the types of content they prefer. These are used to create your list of content activities.

Here are some examples of content activities:

- Blog posts on your site or another company's site
- Articles placed on your site and in industry publications (on- or offline)
- Webinars and other online events
- Podcasts (being a guest on others' and/or through your own)
- Emails to your database or co-marketing with databases from other businesses

When you move to measuring success and iterating on what future expectations are, you'll set "plan" numbers against each activity. For example:

- Blog (ours)—two posts per month
- Guest Blog—one post per month

You will want to make a schedule of posts or any ongoing marketing you are planning to do.

Pick Measurable Key Performance Indicators

In Phase Five (Optimization), key performance indicators (KPIs) are covered in depth, because marketing and sales activities must be measurable. We've all made the mistake of setting KPIs that we simply can't measure. If you do so, you'll be unable to determine whether your product narratives and/or content marketing are working. I mention this now to make you aware, as you work through the marketing process, that you will need to use measurable KPIs for all marketing activities. So, for each marketing activity, you want to ensure you've recorded a response when it occurs (example, clicks through to the blog posts).

If a prospect in your ideal customer profile reads one piece of your content and another prospect reads ten pieces of your content, which prospect is more likely to buy from you? As you may have guessed, the second prospect, since they have demonstrated an affinity for your narratives.

The goal is to have a potential customer engage with your content. To read or listen, watch or experience, and then to demonstrate interest through continued engagement, which creates another measure for us called "propensity to buy" (PTB). This means, if the prospect has a high PTB, they are more likely to buy from you.

This is also known as lead scoring. We need a scoreboard that indicates who has digested what content and how much of it they've consumed. For simplicity (because this is getting complicated), let's give a score of 1 for each blog or podcast engaged by the prospect. If Rita from Acme Corp (a prospect in your ideal customer profile) engages with three pieces of content, we might decide that is enough for Sales to make contact.

GTM is always (not just in the very beginning of the lifecycle) composed of three steps: plan, execute, and iterate. All three steps are critical.

All right! Now you have your product narratives (iterated every three months), and you have specific content marketing activities that you will test each month (plan, actual, difference). As prospects engage, you are building up an individual "score" for them. In essence, you will see which prospects engage the most and are your best bet to reach out to.

Proof That Demand Generation Is Working

According to Dr. Stephen R. Covey, all things are created twice—first in the mind and then in the real world. Physical creations follow mental ones, like homes built according to blueprints. To make your deepest desires a reality, you first need to see and understand what those desires are. So, in short, as we have discussed all throughout this book, beginning with the end in mind is so important. You want to visualize your life, career, or a specific project in the way you want it to turn out before you actually begin pursuing it. The question I get asked more than anything is, "How? How is it possible that you do all these things?" Well, this is how! When you make this conscious effort, you take much greater control over your circumstances or, in this case, your buyers.

Your foundational GTM strategy leads to scored engagement with your content, website, or product from prospective buyers. When the prospect has engaged with enough content, meeting a predetermined score threshold that your teams will decide upon in advance, the software will drop the prospective buyer into your relationship management software and— *boom*! Your lead generation machine is up and running. This warm lead is now familiar with your startup and product(s) and has shown a level of interest that alerts your teams, and primes both the sales representative and lead for a successful sales pipeline process. I call this exercise the "mindset shift." With even more advanced programs, there's endless room to nerd out and refine data points from conversation rates to content engagement percentages; getting into the weeds of a successful customer journey to find opportunities for further insight or streamlining can be very exciting!

Mindset Shift

Everyone has a mindset, and sometimes it needs to shift. When I did one of my annual quests, I faced this head-on. At the time, I was looking out over a two-thousand-foot drop with a parachute in my hand, getting ready to BASE jump off a cliff. Since my mind has always been my greatest challenge, I've come to understand the power of the mind.

Your mind can be shifted in many directions. This is often the case with customers who have a mindset and, like me, do not want to be pushed into buying something . . . or, in this case, off a cliff. You can't push your prospects. Push sales have proven repeatedly that such a strategy doesn't work, and in the odd chance they do, the data says that those prospects have a ten times greater chance of churn. (Customer "churn" is the percentage of customers that stop using your company's product or service during a certain time frame. You can calculate churn rate by dividing the number of customers you lost during that time period—say a quarter—by the number of customers you had at the beginning of that time period.)

The reality is that you can spend ten times more money trying to create mindset shifts over ten Zoom calls, or you can pull customers to you by providing meaningful content focused on your target persona. By letting quality content do the work of the ten Zoom calls, the customer is making their own decision, rather than being pushed. Using the natural path of least resistance and providing them with value will most often drive them to you. In other words, they change their mindset and want to buy what you are selling. When I BASE jumped, I used the landscape and the moment of energy to shift my mindset. I then jumped when I was ready by first getting my mind shift and then being proactive. Like Stephen Covey says, "There's a mental, or first creation, and a physical or second creation to all things." And as I've learned, people don't like having someone else push them to create a mindset shift.

In order to make a mindset shift in our buyers, particularly those who are already set in their ways of doing (or buying) something, we need to try to shift their way of thinking. For example, if you're an iPhone customer and we're trying to sell you an Android, it will require a mindset shift. To do this effectively, you need to understand where they are currently (and why) and where we would like to take them (and why). It's the old "current state" versus "desired future state" scenario. By embracing the principle of beginning with the end in mind, we can answer two questions to develop a high-converting campaign:

- What does a buyer need to *learn* in order to feel pride at the end of their journey?
- What does a buyer need to *see* in order to make a mindset shift?

Answers to these can be as simple as creating a formula for *teaching* the buyer about the return on investment (ROI) associated with purchasing your product or service, then *showing* ROI evidence in a similar business or providing them with customer references that highlight success.

To create an individual propensity to buy score, the prospect has to be present in your customer relationship management (CRM) software. This happens either by manually entering that person (name, business, and email address) or by them "registering" with you for additional content. If a lead or prospect asks for a call, then call them! If they don't, then you will ask them for a call when the score tells you they are ready. By repeatedly testing and assessing your scoring rubric and conversion rates, you'll be able to home in on the right score threshold for your startup.

For example, let's pick a score of 3, based upon the number of engagements with your content. Once a lead has engaged with three pieces of content from you, crossing that predetermined threshold, they are designated as a marketing qualified lead (MQL). This means that, based upon your tested marketing strategy, they are qualified to move to the sales lead assessment process.

MQL Scoring Threshold

The lead is then passed to Sales (usually through a CRM process). Sales will re-qualify the lead:

- Do they want to engage with sales representatives?
- Do they align with your ideal customer profile (ICP)?
- Do they have a real need that can be solved by your product?

If Sales accepts the lead from Marketing, we call this a sales-qualified lead (SQL). This is important, because it confirms that your marketing strategy and team are functioning properly and delivered a qualified lead to your sales representatives. This is a *huge* step in your success!

Once Sales takes the lead, it will enter the sales pipeline, where sales pipeline management will take the baton to handle the SQL.

Sales Process and Management

Sales pipeline management strategy is primarily focused on moving prospects through the different phases, from SQL to purchase. You'll typically have fields associated with each phase, including type, status, contract value, probability, and estimated close date, which come together to provide you with a weighted pipeline value. Before we get to the specifics that you'll use to assemble your strategy, let's review a few of the general principles:

1. Every lead transfer from Marketing to Sales must be through a measurable action in the CRM (like a conversion from lead to prospect or transfer of an account). It should not be done manually.
2. Once a lead reaches Sales, it immediately becomes part of the sales pipeline with a predefined pipeline phase.
3. Each pipeline phase in the CRM must have defined entry/exit criteria and required sales actions. These should be recorded and socialized across your organization.

4. Each pipeline phase in the CRM must have a weighted probability to close. For example, when a lead moves from Marketing to Sales (MQL to SQL), the probability might be 5 percent. When the lead moves to the next pipeline phase (because exit criteria were met), the weighting might move to 25 percent.

You need to work closely with the CEO, as well as the heads of Sales and Marketing and IT, to ensure that your process is measurable. It has to be able to create meaningful reporting that not only forecasts results, but gives you data to make decisions and share them with your investors. You should expect to iterate and optimize your pipeline strategy, and you need quality data to do that.

For example, the reporting you have in place should allow you to understand:

SALES PIPELINE REPORTING INSIGHTS

- **How much revenue do you expect to have in 6 months?**

- **How many sales do you need to hit your goal?**

- **How many marketing activities are required to hit that revenue number?**

To get there, we need to start with some basic data and then make some calculations as assumptions before we iterate based on reality.

For example:

- **Annual Contract Value (ACV).** Let's start with $30,000 as our annual contract value.

- **Ideal Customer Profile (ICP).** We have this well defined, including having an understanding of where our prospects like to look for information (watering holes).

- **Customer Goals.** We want to sign five customers per month at $30,000 each to reach our revenue goals.

- **Leads Needed.** We need to generate enough marketing qualified leads (MQLs) to generate five new customers per month. We'll assume this takes ten leads per sale, so we need fifty active leads each month to reach our goal.

- **Narrative and Content Activities.** We've thoughtfully selected narratives, and we expect each content activity to generate five leads, so we'll need at least ten activities to get our fifty leads (MQLs). Each activity that is complete needs to be recorded for reporting.

- **Scoring.** Implement scoring by using website links that tell your relationship management system when an individual has read your content. Each piece of content gets a score of 1. When the individual reaches a score of 3, we'll move them to Sales. Your chosen number might be lower or higher, depending on your product and the ideal customer profile. Note if you make your number 1, your sales team will be reaching out to everyone who reads even one of your blogs, articles, and so on, which they may have done while in the course of searching for something else. This can take up a lot of your sales team's time. Look for a number (score) of at least 2 or 3.

- **Propensity to Buy.** When the score reaches your target number, the lead is determined to have a strong propensity to buy (PTB) and is moved to Sales. This again needs to be recorded by the relationship management software and it is important that this is a very obvious action to both Sales and Marketing. Expect iterations here.

- **Sales Pipeline.** Break your sales pipeline into phases, which will include entry and exit criteria (entry is a score that tells you they are likely to buy and exit criteria is some action by Sales that signals the sale process is moving forward). Phases also represent action by Sales, but also signals from the prospect that they are moving forward toward a purchase.

Let's give some examples of sales pipeline phases:

- **In Queue**—Marketing has delivered the MQL, and Sales has not yet had a conversation. I'm going to weigh the likelihood of the lead becoming a customer (at the above annual customer value) at 0 percent. This is because I don't yet know if they are truly interested, and I recommend being conservative until the numbers tell you something different.
- **Discovery**—This phase means the lead is now an SQL because Sales is in a conversation about the prospect's need (and again, I would need that to be documented). Do they have a real need for your solution? Do they believe in the value? Can they afford your solution at the annual customer value? I'm going to weigh discovery at 10 percent of ACV (annual contract value). So now I can report on future revenue. If I have fifty prospects at 10 percent, I can forecast five customers.
- **Deal Structure**—Prospect agrees they can afford and wants your solution. We agree on all the terms of the relationship. We want to ensure that they will be happy if this deal is done. Before moving to an agreement, I want every agreement term discussed and resolved. I'm going to weigh this phase at a 50 percent pipeline rating, because we are talking contract specifics, and I know they want to buy.

- **Agreement Pending**—In deal structure, we agreed to all the contract terms. Then we request the contract and send it to the prospect. The prospect is moved to "agreement pending." I'm going to give this a 90 percent pipeline weighting. This means I expect 90 percent of the prospects in this phase to become paying customers. If my failure rate in this phase is greater than 10 percent, then I probably didn't finish my work in earlier phases.

- **Onboarding**—After the contract, we move to onboard our new customer. Weighting should be at 100 percent, unless you have a complicated onboarding process that creates surprises for the customer. If you have any loss of revenue at this phase, you are doing something wrong, and you need to diagnose and fix it immediately.

Go-to-Market–Alignment

Training as a bullfighter taught me that once you step into the ring, it's game on! There is no turning around or the bull will be in a perfect position to knock you out of the ring. The same is true about your product if you go-to-market (GTM) without the alignment of your full team. You will not have time to get aligned after the customers start to flow, and you could end up staring at the horns of angry customers.

Alignment Is Critical in the GTM Phase

Remember, a go-to-market strategy is a plan that helps you define your ideal customers, coordinate your messaging, and position your product for launch. Once you have completed your narratives, content marketing strategy, and sales pipeline management strategy, you are more than halfway toward a successful GTM.

You must ensure your KPIs are in place and the rest of your organization can support all the demand you've generated.

A good GTM strategy also keeps key business units aligned on the same plan, allowing you to meet a market need and effectively iterate on your product. Business units are the people and departments that help bring the product to market, like IT, Legal, Marketing, and Finance. If you don't have alignment between all the departments building your product, it won't matter how great your marketing is or how much you sell.

> ### Small Teams and Departments Are Typical for Startups
>
> When we talk about teams and departments throughout the early phases, this does not mean large teams of ten or twenty people. In fact, at the beginning, you and your partner may make up some of the teams yourself. As your business grows, you will bring in more people, but most startup teams/departments in these early days consist of only a few people, with some overlap. What's good about remaining lean, besides a lower overhead, is that you can be very agile when necessary. Remember, it's easier to quickly turn a kayak around than a cruise liner.

Startups cannot afford to focus only on sales and marketing when they are bringing a product to market. Startups need what is called "cross-functional alignment," which means every functional area of the startup must clearly understand the North Star, vision, and narratives around the product. Recent world events have accelerated the need massively, with more distributed teams and a wider spread customer base, meaning there has never been a better time to make revenue a process. With the world changing at a quicker pace than ever before, customer journeys are becoming increasingly more complex. With more options, more channels, and more touch points, it's harder than ever to remain agile. Lack of alignment across go-to-market teams is one of the biggest instances hurting growth and business outcomes.

An effective revenue process improves agility and provides those key revenue-generating teams with the real-time knowledge they need to inform, act, and create revenue. This mindset evolution is a competitive advantage in a crowded market space and focuses in on:

- People, by aligning your teams around single goals and targets
- Data, by better connecting your tech-stacks
- Processes, by streamlining what you do across the business

According to HubSpot research, organizations with strong alignment deliver 38 percent higher sales win rates and 24 percent faster revenue growth over three years.[6] Without alignment, this acceleration is not possible; not to mention, capital is wasted.

Aligning Your Functional Areas and Shared Services

In the startup world, I've found that a common mistake in the Go-to-Market phase is believing that your validation process only involves functional areas of the business, like Sales and Marketing. While those functional areas are the primary instigators of change, *every* functional area participates in ensuring that your startup's GTM is successful. Let's walk through how the GTM might affect each functional area.

---

6. Leslie Ye, "Sales-Marketing Alignment Increases Revenue by 208% [Infographic]," Hubspot.Com, July 28, 2017, https://blog.hubspot.com/sales/sales-marketing-alignment-increases-revenue-infographic.

IT Services

IT will work closely with Sales and Marketing to build out the GTM delivery and reporting systems. IT will also be tasked with implementing knowledge bases, CRM reporting, customer ticketing, support systems, and all the integrations required to produce KPI reporting. More customers mean every functional area is defining and redefining their customer support and handoff process, all at the same time.

The objective of IT Services should be to provide a solution to manage functional area handoffs in a way that generates the data you need to report on your KPI stacks, which we'll delve into in Phase Five (Optimization). At this point, the focus of GTM is still on *effective* work, not *efficient* work. Therefore, we don't need to spend time automating complicated processes, but we do need visibility. Keep the number of systems small, don't expect systems to interoperate as efficiently as you'd like, but ensure your reporting is in place.

HR Services

HR should prepare for growth and the ability to scale staff in the areas where your startup has the most need. For example, what needs to happen if you want to hire twenty people in three months? What if you need to hire an engineer in another country? HR should assume the GTM will be successful, so they will need to understand how to answer questions such as these and what will be required to achieve the solutions.

Finance

Finance should start with KPIs and ensure all departments have enough data to report on the selected KPIs. Finance should work with IT to ensure that the KPI reporting is accurate. As the GTM progresses, you'll also start to see spending in new areas, and it is important that Finance keeps your monthly financials and runway projections updated.

Relative to the GTM, it is critical that Finance has strong input and veto power of KPI interpretation or whether a KPI is *actually* being achieved. You can't let the fox (in this case Sales) guard the henhouse (whether your GTM KPIs are being achieved or not). You may also start hearing about a need for more staff from each functional area. More customers means everyone feels overworked! You want to keep your startup effective, but don't hire until you start looking at processes that are starting to develop. Make easy efficiency decisions before raising head count.

Legal Services

Legal may have created an agreement or two already, but they need to be prepared for faster turnaround times, especially regarding customer redlines and sales contract approval. You should start to measure agreement turnaround time as Legal's primary KPI. Every day that a customer wants to pay, but can't because the agreement isn't completed, costs you money in terms of lost revenue and burn. At this phase (GTM), you should be actively trying to determine what items in your agreements cause a need for revisions and slow the process so you can remove them.

Finally, it is important for Legal to work with Sales to ensure that all terms in the agreement are discussed with the prospect prior to an agreement being issued. The last thing you want is an agreement that doesn't match a prospect's understanding of core issues. For the most part, when a contract is sent, it should be ready to be signed.

At this point, you should have marketing and sales software in place. However, it still relies on your sales strategy. Throughout all of Phase Three (GTM), you're creating, testing, and iterating on your marketing and sales strategies. The data you gather now will change your future actions. The entire process must be grounded in systems that report on your actions along the way.

Aligning Service Delivery

Service and support are the framework you establish and utilize to provide services to your clients. It is a functional area that is typically the next in line to be impacted by your GTM, as well as the next interaction point for customers.

As your GTM progresses and customer numbers grow, it is vital that your service and support rises to the challenge. Retention is now going to become one of Service and Support's primary KPIs. Do *not* throw employees (effectively, *money*) at retention issues. Focus on listening to your customers, providing effective and proactive support, and consistent issue resolution processes. The goals at this phase are retention alongside referenceable customers.

Process is the key to success when it comes to service and support. Break down your approach into proactive and reactive customer activities, which effectively divides service and support in two sub-functional areas, which we call "customer success" (proactive efforts) and "customer support" (reactive efforts). Proactive customer *success* anticipates what the customers need to be wildly successful using your product and delivers it before the customer asks. Reactive customer *support*, including technical support, billing, support tickets, and general help, is provided *in response* to customer requests. These approaches both belong in service and support, but they will have different staffs (eventually), systems, and processes.

Closely related to process adjustments is ensuring that you are tracking the correct KPIs and metrics for both areas of service and support. To start, it is important to track time spent directly on support versus success. A high volume of support work means something needs to be improved for the customer. This might be more accessible documentation to help the customer self-serve or developing a better user experience and interface. A good product design should be the first line of defense against support requests. No one ever taught you to use the iPhone; you just figured it out. If your customers cannot figure out how to use the product or service, it is not a customer support issue; it is a product and engineering issue. These costs will only multiply as the number of customers grows. While Service and Support should plan for a temporary surge in support work due to your GTM, it should communicate effectively with Product and Engineering (maybe other departments, as well) to resolve what is causing customers to reach out for support.

The most effective way of creating this link is to ensure all support activities are documented in a ticketing system. This simply means that you can record an issue, track it to a customer, record time spent on the issue, and tally up similar issues as feedback for the product. Many versions of customer relationship management software now have some limited ticketing features. You don't need a fancy system yet, just enough to stay organized. But do invest in the process around support because customers leave if there are real support issues that are not addressed. Retention and progress are the heart of support.

Customer Success plans for success. You need to understand what you can do to make the customer experience wildly successful. What does success mean for them? What do they need to know or do that turns a standard user into a power user and one who sees success in their own KPIs? What are your customer's KPIs? You have to know the answers to these types of questions before you can make your customers successful.

Measuring customer satisfaction score (CSAT) includes onboarding time and time to value (TTV), which refers to the *time* it takes for a user to realize the expected *value* from your product. Start learning what makes one customer feel successful and another feel underserved.

The key to customer success is being *proactive*. The customer shouldn't call you to ask how they can get onboarded—you should call the customer automatically based on a trigger in your sign-up process. Customer Success must proactively engage with the customer to learn what they want to accomplish and provide that support before they ask.

Aligning Product and Engineering

The primary objective of the product and engineering functional areas during your GTM is continuing to refine the product by listening to customer feedback in every form, and across every channel.

Product and Engineering will very quickly need to formalize a process to capture and process feedback. No matter how beautiful or perfect you believe your product is at the start of your GTM, you *will* get a lot of unexpected feedback that you didn't hear from your user advisory board. Why? Because customers tell you different things than prospects.

Your user advisory board members will often look past, or not notice, inefficiencies in the implementation, because they are being asked about the end goal or value of the product. But your customers will tell you the truth about that ugly color scheme or that your log-out process doesn't seem right.

It is vitally important that Product and Engineering have the correct attitude regarding customer feedback. It is a gift given by a user who cares enough to try and help your product improve. The only thing worse than a customer providing feedback is a customer not caring enough about your product to even bother providing feedback. Engaged users are retained users—do them justice by acting on their feedback meaningfully, respectfully, and quickly.

That said, there are different kinds of feedback that should be prioritized and acted upon accordingly. Not every customer request will fit your product vision, and not every bug is a five-alarm fire. The best way to work through the ambiguous nature of feedback is to hold a consistent weekly or biweekly meeting where the product and engineering teams work with the service and support teams and other functional areas to better understand the context of a certain piece of feedback.

The faster your feedback loop between your customer and your product and engineering team, the faster the sales and marketing team will be able to test new product narratives or content marketing strategies.

Fail Fast and Triumph

As Kipling says, "To really make it in life, you've got to learn to meet with triumph and disaster and treat those two imposters just the same."

Getting your GTM strategy right is a bit like that. If you're too quick to assume you've triumphed and found a winning approach, you'll risk putting too much of your startup on the line with an unproven strategy. And if you get despondent when things don't work out the first time around, you'll wind up crashing instead of using the opportunity to reinvigorate your marketing and find a path forward.

It's very easy for visionaries to get carried away with what they're seeing at a surface level. I once had an entrepreneur that I was working with who had an extraordinary vision for a clothing line, hoping to break some ground in the realm of fashion entrepreneurialism. She dove in headfirst, allowing her vision to guide her through the design process, acquiring warehouses, and moving forward with manufacturing . . . only for her to launch an amazing-looking product that customers hated. What gets lost in this waterfall strategy, fueled solely by vision, is the time and money poured into a product that has no guarantee of customer satisfaction. Her clothes looked marvelous, but the fabric was a big issue. If this entrepreneur hadn't stayed holed up behind that wall and, instead, had designed a few garments to allow a group of testers to try and offer feedback on, she could have then gone back in to make adjustments. Her clothing would have had the benefits of her artistic vision while ensuring that the actual material from which they were created was comfortable for her customer base. These are mistakes from which many startups cannot afford to bounce back.

A startup I founded, called AdAssured, spun out of the ecosystem I had developed and maintained for Affiliate Traction. Watching the ecosystem evolve to the compliance of affiliates, I saw a problem and an opportunity. The idea was selling software that could take what was a manual process of affiliate compliance and use crawling and data feeds to find violators. We could then create a case in a platform, add the policies of the program, and find violations. Later, this process was automated for the most part, creating a safer marketing channel, which, in turn, allowed the sector to attract more brand-conscious merchants who had previously been afraid of damage to the brand. Sounds good, right? Well, it did end up working out; however, I missed a few important data points relative to the market when I did the North Star (which I have since updated). I soon realized that, even though the total addressable market (TAM) and the total serviceable market (TSM) looked good, the total obtainable market (TOM) was a very different thing.

This was highlighted in my initial GTM KPIs. Sure, every affiliate network, performance marketing team, agency, and brand might theoretically be a potential buyer solution. But, in reality, my GTM would only let me reach a much smaller subset of the sector because the industry was still evolving, and many brands were not even aware of this challenge. I needed to educate them about the problem and then sell them the solution by adding another moving part to the GTM.

Obviously, that reality check was disappointing, but I was lucky. It came before I'd gone out and tried to raise money to grow. I was able to adjust my expectations and turn my startup into something smaller but a lot more stable. The startup sold to one of the top three performance marketing networks in the world. The point is, when you look at missteps along the way, you can either see potential disaster or, if looking through the right lens, you can see that missteps followed by course corrections aren't disappointing. In fact, learning and thriving from such errors or failures is actually pretty exhilarating. This is very common in the world of startups, so expect that you will need to make changes along the way. Before you give up on an idea that didn't pan out as you had expected, look at every possibility—try many lenses. Sometimes learning to ward off despondency is the hardest part of a GTM strategy—but in many ways, it's the most important part. There's a degree of scaling down of ambition as you bring your vision in line with reality.

At this phase (GTM) in the startup's growth, you still have absolute license to goof, mess up, make mistakes, misread the marketplace, and come back stronger than ever—because you're using all of these mistakes as *learning opportunities.*

This freedom to make mistakes and still push through won't last much longer, so enjoy it—and exploit it—while you can. As the saying goes, nothing sells like success. So, make your mistakes in private, and use them to build the staircase that will carry you to the firmer ground that you can use as a platform for growth.

Once you've finally proven your marketing strategy, take the opportunity to flex a little. Don't tell your investors about your mistakes—brag about your successes and bring receipts to show that your strategy really does do everything you're promising. When you can show that you've got what it takes to succeed, nobody will ever point to, or even remember, all those missteps you took along the way. Years later, you can put them in your book, or at least have some good stories at cocktail hours.

Your investors only care about end results. Once you've solved a Rubik's Cube, nobody cares how many times you had to twist it and re-twist it—they're just impressed by all those one-color 3X3 grids, neatly on display.

In the same way, if you can turn up with hard data that proves your GTM strategy is a minimum viable product, nobody will worry about how many iterations you went through before you hit the motherlode. All they'll care about is that you're ready to launch and ready to grow. And that's exactly what we'll cover in the next chapter with the Standardization phase.

Once your adjustments are made, your KPIs are telling you more, and your functional teams are ready, hit the market. Be conservative and expect iterations.

You must be able to launch into the market (messaging and tactic), win customers (mindset shift and sales), service customers (onboarding and retention), and continue product development in a profitable way.

Warning: If you cannot see a profit on the table, you cannot move forward. *Running out of cash is the number one reason that startups fail.*

Always Stay Agile When Going to Market

Focusing on flexibility throughout the GTM phase allows project teams to respond quickly to new insights or changes in the project scope or deliverables. Being agile, or flexible, involves multiple short rounds of development, after which the project stakeholders evaluate the work and adjust their plans based on any new information that may have come to light. The ultimate goal is to deliver higher quality products on shorter timelines, with less need for extensive rework or revision.

It's often helpful to think about your go-to-market (GTM) as its own lifecycle—you'll pass from one objective to the next, iterating your way to a marketing strategy that delivers the goods. But sometimes, things get more complicated. What if, for instance, your data causes you to rethink the nature of your product? That happens more often than you'd think, even after a successful product validation process.

Sometimes, a product can work incredibly well but be incredibly hard to sell to the persona. In such a case, you have little choice but to add a big recursive loop to your GTM flow chart and head back to the product-development phase armed with the new information you've gathered.

To formally move on to Phase Four (Standardization) and get validation, ensure that you've completed what I call the GTM stack, which includes the following:

Customer and Persona

- Ideal customer profile, which tells you about the company.
- Persona, which tells you about the person you have to convince at the company.
- Customer Journey, which tells you where they go for information (watering holes), what they are looking for (topics), and why they are looking (motivation).

Content Strategy

- North Star, which gives you your narrative spine.
- Narrative spine, which gives you your topics.
- Topics, which give you your content.

Content Syndication Strategy

- Using your customer journey and the "watch, listen, read, experience" format, decide on where you will place the various types of content. This includes all social platforms, email, blog, and website.

Advertising Strategies

- Earned or organic advertising in search, social, display.
- Paid advertising in search, social, display.

Sales Strategies

- Premium, free trial, limited access, loss leader.
- Sales process and management.

Functional Area Alignment

- Product and Engineering quick iterations and customer listening.
- Shared Services (IT, HR, Finance, Legal).
- Service and Support—implementing an agile process to capture feedback.
- Key Performance Indicators (KPIs).
- Data capture and KPI stack management.

If, and only if, you can confidently answer yes to completing all of the above are you ready to move on to Phase Four in the Startup Science Lifecycle, which is Standardization. Regardless of whether you've decided to keep your startup as is, or continue to expand, the next step is to standardize all that you've learned to create a stable, repeatable startup model.

CHAPTER WRAP-UP

At this point, you'll have completed your initial go-to-market testing and validated parts, if not all your vision. You're also likely in a position to raise your series seed round and begin to standardize every part of your startup. It's likely been anywhere from six months to two years since you've completed Phase Two (Product).

Phase Four: Standardizing for Competitive Advantage

If you think of standardization as the best that you know today, but which is to be improved tomorrow, you get somewhere.

–Henry Ford

Have you met Bob? You know, Bob, the *only one* in your startup or department that knows how to run that report you need, how a customer's account works, or even where the template is for running performance reports? You get the idea.

Well, Bob just got a new job and has decided to leave your lovely startup today with no prior notice. As happy as you are for Bob, this puts you and your startup in a tough spot. You now need to understand *exactly* what Bob's documented and undocumented responsibilities were in order to hire and train a replacement. You need the ins and outs, the when, the where, the who, and the how. In essence, Bob has the key to the vault, and you need it. At best, you can have Bob, who has lost interest and is preoccupied with excitement over his new job, haphazardly cross-train an existing busy employee, which adds a huge distraction to the team and leaves an existing team member with gaps in knowledge. At worst, Bob has already said sayonara, and the small things—that can spiral into big things—slowly emerge like drops of rain before the much bigger rainstorm. If he's not the one there to address them, the drops of water will slowly fill the work bucket until there's an overflow or leak that crashes the entire operation. It's only now that you realize how valuable Bob was to your company.

I've been through this situation, and it's not fun! It's unfortunately an inevitable reality that every one of us will encounter during our careers.

What Is Standardization?

Standardization is the process by which a company makes its methods and processes uniform throughout its organization. In essence, it's a guidebook to what Bob was doing successfully all this time at your company. It is the logical systems put in place to streamline every process in your workday. Rather than taking each situation as it arises, you react according to a set list of instructions and protocols. The goal is to make sure a system is in place that allows actions to be performed universally, meaning you are not overly reliant on one person, or even one team, to perform a task, action, or explain a system, project, sales technique, and so on.

Standardization results in action taken that generates a proven business result. This is important because having different approaches to various situations within a company may ultimately translate into a lack of control. Standardization in companies is meant to achieve cost savings, increase customer satisfaction, and improve competitiveness, no matter the channel used or country of purchase. It also means that turnover in your business (as in Bob leaving) does not create a flood of problems and issues that dilute productivity.

The Power of Standardization

When I first sold Affiliate Traction, I had already implemented standardized best practices across my startup—and it quickly emerged that my teams were generating five times more revenue per employee than in teams where no such standards or processes were in place. That was obvious as soon as you walked into a meeting. For starters, the teams that lacked standardized best practices were holding far more meetings, because they constantly had to figure things out on the fly and come up with solutions from scratch every time problems cropped up.

The *other* giveaway was that it seemed like nobody could sit still for the entire length of a meeting. Every time I sat in, I'd see phones pinging and people dashing off to deal with some new crisis that had just cropped up. This is typical of the "choose your own adventure" mode of running a startup: everyone thinks the problems they're encountering are unique, and everyone's trying to solve them from scratch.

When you're working with standardized best practices, on the other hand, everyone knows their problems *aren't* unique, and that, in fact, there's a rule book already in place to tell them how to handle the crisis du jour. That means there are far fewer fires to put out, because everyone is doing the important things to prevent the urgent things from rearing their ugly heads. Everyone knows what they're doing and how to solve any problems they encounter.

I want to emphasize that best practices for mundane problems allow you the space and time to pursue new opportunities or deal with legitimate problems. The times when genuinely new problems emerge are fairly rare, and even then, it's typically possible to extend an existing best practice to solve the crisis pretty quickly.

This is a lesson I learned in my research talking to the smokejumpers, the Navy SEAL equivalent of a fireman. In my home state of California, wildfires are a huge issue, and the fire departments here are outright amazing. Sitting down with the fire chief, in his perfectly organized office that was so clean you could eat off the floor, I asked him, "How do you go about putting out a wildfire?"

He laughed and said, "We don't."

I must have looked pretty confused.

He clarified, "The goal isn't to *put out* the fire. It's to contain it and stop it from getting any bigger. Only after we've contained it do we start thinking about how to put it out—and that's an easy task, because once it's contained, it's going to burn itself out pretty soon in any case."

"How is this done?" I asked.

"Let's say the area is a square. We build a fire road, which is a strip of land that has been cleared or plowed with fire-resistant vegetation to prevent a fire from spreading. Once that is in place and the fire eats up all the fuel and burns itself out, then it is contained."

"I see. But it must be difficult to let fires burn," I replied.

He explained, "If we keep trying to put out all the fires, while we are putting one out, another one would be right behind us. So we stay focused on containing all of the fires first and letting them burn themselves out."

Startups that fail to put effective best practices in place, including standardization, wind up focusing on putting out fires, instead of creating environments where they can prevent, control, and contain the fires. A startup without best practices is guaranteed to always have fires, because as soon as one fire is out, another will have started somewhere else. The end result is always a group of people who can't focus on anything—and especially not growth and scalability—because they're so busy running from one crisis to the next.

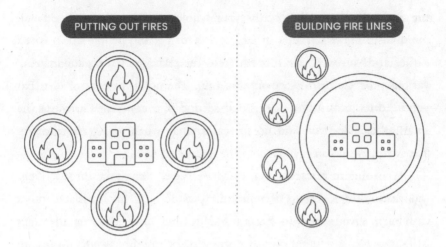

At Affiliate Traction, we applied the best-practices approach across the teams I worked with and managed to reduce the average employee onboarding time from seven months to just thirty days, ensuring that everyone on every team was pulling their weight while driving growth. That all boils down into a scalable and replicable (standardized) pathway to success.

Another example is the way Affiliate Traction standardized employee onboarding. Instead of having employees operate at 20 percent productivity for their first month, then 30 percent in their second, and so on, making only incremental gains as they gradually learned the ropes, Affiliate Traction was able to get people up to speed *fast*, and have them firing on all cylinders within thirty to sixty days.

Standardization helps you by eliminating distractions, waste, and costly mishaps—and if you bake these optimizations in early on, while you're still scaling up, you'll be that much more likely to succeed.

Lack of Standardization Bleeds Cash

Consider this: If you're paying someone $10,000 a month to work at 20 percent of their capacity, you're effectively pouring $8,000 a month down the drain. Replicate that across your whole organization, and you will bleed cash. Have a standardized process for getting people up to speed earlier and you will save money later. The same goes for standardizing various processes across the organization. The point, of course, isn't that you need to account for every single second of every day. Rather, it's the small efficiencies that add up to real savings when you scale them up across your workforce.

According to research from Business Wire, it can take three to eight months for employees to become fully productive. This translates into a cash burn. If your new hire starts at $120K fully burdened, annually that's $10K/month. If it takes only five months, or roughly twenty weeks, to train your new hire, that costs you $476 per day, not including recruiting fees of 20 percent of the first-year wages. The cost of growth is substantial, and the biggest part is head count, and the majority of that in the first year is training, which is broken down into learning the industry, the business, and the job.

Now let's add just one more layer to this to really make the point about the significance of standardization and best practices. When you go to exit your business, the acquirer will want to know, in regard to diligence, how your business operates. To make this point, I'll use my favorite example. Try to put together a car motor without instructions; it's easier than getting a startup off the ground. If you have never tried, let me explain. There are quite a few parts that go together in a very specific order, and only in that order, and if you get it wrong, you'll find yourself taking it apart to try again and again.

Handing over your business to an acquirer without best practices is like handing over a crate of motor parts with no instructions. I had a company go all the way through, just to get to the part where diligence focused on how the business ran. They were going over performance and head count costs when they discovered that the founder had not kept up with standardization. The deal was paused for six months, and by that time, the situation had changed. The acquirer had slipped in another acquisition and now needed time to digest the new purchase. This stretched out the exit and dragged the leadership of the company through a lengthy process. In the end, it was a close call, but the deal did, in fact, go through, but for much less than expected due to penalties assessed for the cost of documenting how the company ran. For a while, the situation was touch-and-go, which presented so much distraction that, if the deal had not gone through, it might have killed the company. Had there been a standardized process by which the founder was keeping the data as she should have been doing, this would have been a much quicker, easier exit.

Prioritize Standardization

Standardization provides an answer. By ensuring that every functional area and employee has their knowledge documented and standardized, you reduce the risk that any one individual owns intellectual or tribal knowledge that, if disappeared, would hurt your business. At the same time, standardization provides a greater ability to hire new employees, run your startup more effectively, and saves you literally millions in startup capital adding to your equity being diluted.

Even though you will have started this earlier, Phase Four remains focused on the simple concept of standardization and the more difficult goal of deploying it in your startup. Up to this point, you've done the hard work of building your North Star, prototyping your way to an MVP, and have had the aspects of your go-to-market tested and validated. Now is the time to ensure each of your functional areas has best practices in place that guarantee high-quality results. You won't have time to build this foundation after entering Phase Five (Optimization) and raising your largest round of funding thus far.

To achieve this, you need to accomplish three objectives:

- Create best practices for your operations.
- Organize a folder structure that is integrated into your best practices.
- Design and implement customer relationship management software and other supporting systems that are integrated into your best practices.

The "Humble" Best Practice

Standardization at its core should be built around a simple tool—the "humble" best practice. You may have heard of this previously as a standard operating procedure (SOP). This is not the same thing. SOPs are most often over-bloated blocks of text written by tech writers. Employee handbooks are also not considered best practices. While often boring, they basically provide a mix of company policies and adhere with laws and ordinances to protect a company from liability. Standardization is a set of best practices that is exactly what it sounds like: a written description of how to accomplish a certain task that anyone can readily understand.

Humble best practices are made up of three simple parts:

- **What**—Accountability: This is the functional area.
- **When**—Timing: When the action actually happens.
- **How**—By using your written best business practices.

It's important to remember this is "plain speak." It is *not* fancy tech talk, or industry terminology. If a newbie can't understand and follow the standardization easily, then it's wrong. Don't overcomplicate this—keep it simple, simple, simple!

Through extensive trial and error, I settled on the following ten guidelines for writing best practices in a straightforward and easily understandable manner.

1. A best practice should be written if an action, interaction, or work process has proven to be effective.

2. Write best practices using the "rule of three," which states: if it has been done successfully in a specific manner three times, write it down to be standardized.

3. Functional leaders should be aware of the need for standardization of various processes in their area of operation. Seek their input when it comes to activities that may need to be standardized.

4. Functional leaders are accountable to approve and deploy best practices.

5. Best practices should be reviewed, approved, and vetted by the functional area leader before being deployed to the startup's knowledge base. (A knowledge base should be Wiki software, or something like that. It must also be easy to use and edit.)

6. The leader must align other functional area leaders so best practices are considered handoffs between departments and so they set other teams up for success.

7. Best practices should contain only the required information in a clear and easily understandable manner. Remember, this is not tech speak or business jargon.

8. Best practices should follow a standard template, which consists of a trigger (when it is performed), the actual detailed best practice itself, and, if applicable, a next step.

9. Best practices should be easily accessible.

10. Best practices should be written only in the startup's knowledge base software, not on local machines.

Best practices allow an organization to operate more effectively, because the day-to-day is documented, transparent, and accessible. Everyone, not just a specific employee or functional area leader, knows how the startup should run.

Best practices will use a folder structure, customer relationship management software, and other systems required for the employee to accomplish the task. These folders will be the instruction manual to use these systems in a way that produces efficiency and the ability to create KPIs.

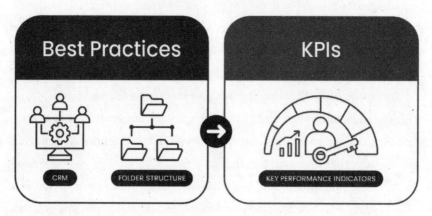

The Folder Structure

Folder structures are often an afterthought. But they are where you store documents of all sorts. These are your plans, your reports, research, and so much more. This is your intellectual property that you will want to leverage. A correctly managed folder structure allows staff to move quickly and effectively. Creating an "afterthought" folder structure is a drag and a serious leak in productivity and information, not to mention a security risk.

Think carefully about your retention of intellectual properties and tribal knowledge. This must be balanced against being able to find what's useful by keeping a tidy folder structure. Give your employees a best practice folder, which ties your best practices to critical documents in the folder structure. Folder structures should generally be molded around your company functional area setup. For example, you should have an area for corporate documents, which is accessible to the C-suite or leaders of functional areas. You can then easily prioritize folders with top-level folders for each of the functional areas. Within those functional area folders, there should be top-level folders for each department. Underneath that, you'll want to determine which standard and unique folders every department should have. Folders, such as templates, reporting, working documents, and many more, are helpful for every functional area.

Don't be too prescriptive. Each department will have their own needs and should have the ability to add the organizational items that they *specifically and frequently* require.

You should also think about access. Some departments have sensitive information, such as Finance, Engineering, or even HR. Not everyone should know exactly how your software is built, so build your drive with access rules in mind. Ideally, you do this by focusing on specific roles in your startup. For example, the head of Finance needs access to specific financial materials, so you can provide them access to specific standardized information. That way, as you onboard new hires, such as a new head of Finance, they have access to all the documents they need, and they can easily access them either directly in the folder structure, or through public best practices.

This also comes into play when you start preparing for an acquisition. An acquirer will need access to a ton of different documentation, both at a corporate level, as well as within each functional area. You don't want to need to scramble to fix that right before diligence. As soon as they request something, you should have it ready. You don't want to delay a transaction due to a messy folder structure.

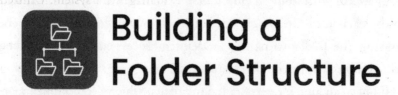

Building a Folder Structure

① Each Functional Area has a folder

② Don't be too prescriptive

③ Control access

In summary, have folders for each functional area, don't be too prescriptive, and control who has access to what.

Customer Relationship Management Software and Other Support Systems

CRM stands for "customer relationship management." It is the heart of your Marketing, Sales, and Service areas. Like the folder system, the CRM stores your intellectual property and business knowledge. Your growth and retention KPIs will be sourced through your CRM. With a poorly implemented and used CRM, your growth and retention will suffer.

CRMs get messy with duplicate accounts, non-updated pipeline values, and workflow. The way your startup uses the CRM is critical to business development, forecasting, marketing, and retention. How to use the CRM (based on each role in your startup) should be documented in best practices. CRMs (and other support systems) are just technology that can be configured to meet your business needs, so do that! Remember to document and standardize how you use the CRM and how you report based on that usage.

CRMs are first and foremost a *contact* management system. Utilized mostly by Sales, Marketing, and Service, they are still used across the company. A CRM can tell you what interactions your teams have had with a prospect or a customer, and whether they were successful or not.

From a random prospect on the Internet, to one of your most important accounts, you can see the entire journey and all the touch points along the way. CRMs can be the ultimate tool in showing off the health of your business. The CRM can forecast what your company will be tomorrow, next month, or even next year. By maintaining a consistent pipeline, you can project potential earnings based on how far along someone is in the process.

This is an invaluable tool when it comes to obtaining investment capital. You can show validation of your product by showing how many people are interested. It's also a map of your sales process, highlighting places of friction or success.

The CRM also serves as a resource for your Marketing department. Have your people focus on reaching people who have legitimate interest or who've shown interest in the past. By having a registrar of customers and leads, Marketing never has to wonder to whom they should market.

Lastly, within the CRM, your service team has a complete picture of a customer. They can see the conversations they've had with Sales, and the content customers responded to in marketing. Any desires or feature requests will be documented, and any problems or successes in the past will also be viewable. Support won't be running blind when talking to a customer. They'll have everything they need to quickly and successfully solve problems.

Nobody Enjoys Standardizing

Through standardization, you'll be able to cut costs, boost productivity, and drive sustainable growth. But there's a catch: standardization is effective, but it isn't sexy. If you've fallen in love with your self-image as a startup visionary, it can be pretty hard to force yourself to buckle down and sweat the details of standardizing startup operations.

I watched this process play out in a growing software startup I'd invested in, after they'd used the prototyping process to figure out their MVP product and their go-to-market strategy. I sat down with the founders and said, "Okay, now it's time to start with standardization, documenting best practices, and getting ready to scale." They were less than thrilled. After all, they'd just *shown* they had a winning product, and *proven* that they had an effective strategy for selling it. Why was I now insisting they sit down and start writing? "Hey, it's a necessary evil," I explained. "Just do it."

Spoiler alert: they didn't do it. Instead, they went out and hired a bunch of promising employees, gave them each a cubicle and a computer, and told them to start handling service calls, while the founders went out and started growing the startup. The results, predictably, were terrible. Without proper support and guidance, the output from the new hires was disastrously bad. In the end, the founders had to cut their losses, fire the new employees, and step back to reevaluate their operational plan. This was certainly not the fault of the new hires. Without the structure that standardization provides, they were tossed into the storm.

In another example, a startup was running KPIs and judging the performance of the teams based on those KPIs. The problem was that everyone was doing things in a slightly different manner, so, obviously, they had different results. They were working in a system that used top-grading, which is a strategy to place individuals and teams in categories. For instance, A Players had the most potential for high performance, followed by B Players and C Players, who might require more work to be successful. The employers asked me why they could not get performances up after having top-graded several times. I asked if they had some kind of best practices to use as comparison. They told me they didn't. In the end, they had no sustainable system for comparing and grading their players. As a result, they were letting go of people, paying recruiter fees, and causing a disruption to the business for no reason. It is simply hard to tell if someone is performing well or doing a good job if there is no way to define what a good job means.

If, for example, you have two people running a mile, and each is taking a different route, would they have the same times? Doubtful. If one runner finished in 10.5 minutes and the other finished in 11 minutes, would that mean the one who had the better time was the better runner? Not necessarily. What if one ran on flat ground and the other on a hill? What if one had more obstacles in their path? Without adequate comparable data, you do not know who ran the better race. You are judging performance, making comparisons, and trying to make improvements based on flawed data.

Having your best practices in place allows you to track correctly, then make decisions based on better data—hence, you are comparing apples to apples. This is not only about top-grading—you may find better ways of doing things that may take longer for this team—but by setting up a data system for determining accurate results, you can focus on the outcome as an element of performance. To drive this point, just like your customers teach you what to build, let your teams teach you how to standardize processes. Give them room, even rewards, and you will see your company improve without force.

Founders, looking slightly sheepish, come to me asking for more working capital in order to hire people whenever they need it. To me, this seems like a budgeting problem. Why do they suddenly need more money? So, I will ask them, "What went wrong?" The founders usually give me the same excuse I hear virtually every time in cases like this: "We were just too busy."

I'll spare you my response, but suffice it to say, founders leave such meetings with a clear understanding that, when it comes to standardization, being too busy isn't an option. To their credit, most will go away and create a clear internal system to document workflows and best practices, and are able to get themselves back on track, and to give their new hires a clear idea of what their job entails and the support they need to grow in the company.

Standardization Produces Customer and Employee Retention

The reality is that managing retention and churn is like trying to fill a leaky bucket. The customers you acquire are like the water you pour in. The more you pour, the quicker the bucket fills. But there's a hole in the bottom, too, and the bigger that hole, the quicker the bucket will drain. In order to fill your bucket, you need to take care of both parts of the equation, and make sure the water you're pouring in doesn't just splash out onto the floor. The lost water is churn, and the water you retain is retention. It costs less to retain your current customers than to constantly seek out new customers. If you fix the hole in the bucket, you'll retain the water and won't have to continually refill it with new water.

Fortunately, the Startup Science Lifecycle helps you learn how to course correct and develop standardized processes in time to stanch the hole at the bottom of the bucket. In the story above, the founders managed to build out the infrastructure and service functions needed to retain customers, employees, and drive scalable growth.

There's a silver lining to this story too. In one situation, when a startup finally achieved their $40M+ exit, it was in large part because of the standardization they'd implemented. As part of their due diligence, their acquirer spent plenty of time looking over the documentation they'd implemented, because seeing that those processes had been properly documented gave the acquirer confidence that the success of the startup would not be a going concern, even if key employees moved on.

No matter how profitable your startup is, or how great your product is, without clear workflows and standard processes, your exit may be delayed or killed.

Bear this in mind: as mentioned earlier, standardizing might not seem cool or exciting, but it's a vital rung in the ladder that leads you to your exit.

CHAPTER WRAP-UP

At this point, you will have completed your initial pass at standardizing each functional area. You have best practices covering the majority of the work your team completes on a regular basis in a location accessible to the entire startup. These best practices become the user manual to your folder structure, CRM, and all other supporting systems required to execute. These systems will produce reliable KPIs, because you've standardized how KPI data is created. And the best practices reduce the time needed to bring new hires to top-graded productivity, allowing you to move faster.

Phase Five: Optimization

Refinement is simply the process of removing unwanted elements providing improvements through small changes, but optimization magnifies those small improvements.

–Albert Einstein

I absolutely love optimization. When I was thirteen, I saw Arnold Schwarzenegger and decided that I wanted to be like him. No more being bullied or pushed around. No one would dare take on Arnold. I learned the concept of what is called "bodybuilding symmetry," which is basically balance. Most people don't know the amount of time body-builders spend trying to get the perfect balance. I am not talking about those you see with large muscles that are out of proportion with the rest of their bodies. I'm talking about *real* bodybuilders that get the highest competitive scores based on their body symmetry. Everything has to be in sync with everything else.

Like most sports and competitions, bodybuilding has a season in which competitions are held. In the offseason, you train for size, and then in the competitive season, you refine, review, and optimize your body. In my first competition, I placed third, penalized for my chest being out of balance, so I spent the next year working on my chest and placed second the following year. For those of us who do this as a sport, this is a never-ending mission of training even the smallest parts for balance. I would spend hours documenting workouts, weights, and many other metrics, then use the data, along with measurements and pictures, to focus on where I needed to refine my body, without letting the rest of the body become out of balance.

When your business gets into the Optimization phase, it's also a never-ending process of evaluation, moving your focus to where it needs to be, and chasing the best possible outcomes based on appropriate metrics. Think of it as a game, one that lets you continuously learn and advance as you go.

Ready to have some fun? Welcome to the Optimization phase, where products get leaner, faster, and better, while margins increase. This is my favorite phase of the Startup Science Lifecycle. It is the process of continuous improvement, in which you utilize your best practices, valuation drivers, and leading and lagging KPIs, to find optimization opportunities to reduce waste and increase margin.

Series-B Round

Startups in Phase Five typically raise their fifth round of external funding, often colloquially known as the series-B round. Series-B capital rounds typically involve investments in the region of $500,000 to $5M, with current startup valuations of around $12M and up.

Kaizen—Continuous Improvement

KPIs form the foundation to operationalize continuous improvement in every startup. Without clear leading and lagging KPIs, your startup is flying blind. But KPIs alone are not enough. You need additional tools for your toolbox to successfully operationalize the changes your KPIs suggest.

Armed with clear empirical deep data, you can apply the concept, or methodology, known as Kaizen, which is a Japanese word meaning "change for better." It also implies a philosophy of continuous improvement. Toyota used this system in their production. It allowed the car company to humanize the workplace and allowed employees to look for areas in which improvement might be needed and/or waste could be eliminated to increase efficiency.

During Phase Five (Optimization), we utilize the Kaizen methodology to find and eliminate waste, which is defined as anything that does not need to be done or can be done more efficiently. This includes eliminating anything that causes distractions, creates context switching, or is the result of what is called the "ratchet effect." This refers to tasks, processes, or action items that have been added over time but not removed. The ratchet effect is essentially stacking topics one on top of the other without considering what's been there and without optimizing to keep the whole stack manageable. This is most common in corporations, who will often add, but not optimize, processes, and other systems. In the end, you'll need an army of people just to manage the ratchet effect. While such additions may have been helpful initially, they are often no longer necessary or applicable to the current state of the startup and should be changed or removed to improve efficiency.

Point Kaizen and Systematic Kaizen

"Point" Kaizen happens very quickly and usually without much planning. As soon as something is found broken or incorrect, quick and immediate measures are taken to correct the issues. These measures are generally small, isolated, and easy to implement. However, they can have a huge impact. It is also possible that the positive effects of point Kaizen in one area can reduce or eliminate benefits of point Kaizen in some other areas. While point Kaizen is initially focused on one functional area, you need to monitor the downstream effects in other functional areas and their departments to ensure a greater ripple has not occurred. Point Kaizen is one of the most commonly implemented types of Kaizen for quick-fix issues.

Systematic Kaizen is accomplished in an organized manner and is devised to address system-level problems in an organization. It is an upper-level strategic planning method that typically takes much longer to operationalize than point Kaizen. Systematic Kaizen is the core of the operating system that I use in the Startup Science Lifecycle because it focuses on a more holistic approach across functional areas. Kaizen starts with the customer's journey and experience. It then adds KPI layers, Net Promoter Scores, and employee Net Promoter Scores feedback layers.

The Five Whys

A tool used in conjunction with point Kaizen is the "five," which is a form of root cause analysis in which the user asks a series of five "why" questions about a failure that has occurred, basing each subsequent question on the answer to the previous. There are normally a series of causes stemming from one root cause, and they can be visualized using fishbone diagrams or tables.

In my experience, it normally takes five iterations to understand and address what's really going on. For example, I'm working on funding a marketing technology startup that recently ran into financial issues for the second time. Essentially, the founders ran out of cash and could not pay back the million dollars they had borrowed to get the startup off the ground.

The first question I asked was simple:

1. Why did this happen? The simplest reason was that they didn't properly forecast their spending or their income.
2. Why not? Because they simply didn't know when the revenue was going to come in.
3. Why? There was nothing in their contracts that indicated when the clients would become active and when they would pay, and there was no KPI to measure cycle-times.
4. Why was that information missing? Because the account manager was onboarding new clients without telling the Finance department that revenue was booked or when it was supposed to come in.
5. Why? Because there was simply no process in place for the two functional areas to communicate.

The 5 Whys

WHY 1 **Why did we lose 1,000 customers last month?**
Because critical bugs were not fixed

WHY 2 **Why were the bugs not fixed?**
Because the bugs were not reported to Engineering

WHY 3 **Why weren't the bugs reported to Engineering?**
Because the bug reporting system was not working

WHY 4 **Why was the bug reporting system not working?**
Because our account with that system was frozen

WHY 5 **Why was our bug reporting account frozen?**
Because the Accounting department failed to pay the quarterly bill for our access to the bug reporting software

ROOT
CAUSE

Similar to reviewing your leading and lagging KPIs versus your plan, the "five whys" method allows you to drill down and identify the root cause of operational issues quickly and efficiently.

Once a startup has gained a deeper understanding of a problem, it's time to make a decision. You can choose to do nothing or do something, even if it could be the wrong choice. The worst course of action at this point is to make no decision because it prevents the organization from learning and moving forward. Even making the wrong decision is better than not taking action, because startups can capitalize on their mistakes, gain valuable knowledge in the process, and continue the process of Kaizen. The reality is that Kaizen itself requires mistakes or failure to learn, and learning is required for progress!

The Valuation Driver and Performance Indicator Stack

First, let's walk through the basics of optimization and what being "data driven" means. Businesses have layers of performance that range from indicators all the way up to your valuation drivers. For our purpose, which is selling your startup, we discuss the significant valuation drivers—growth, margin, and retention—which are all core financial numbers when it comes to your valuation. Let's break these down.

GROWTH

Growth is defined as increasing both the number of customers you have, as well as the revenue you derive from those customers, initially and on a recurring basis. It is an indicator that customers who fit your ideal customer profile (ICP) and are receiving enough value from your product are willing to pay for it initially and on an ongoing basis. To an acquirer, new and existing sales growth tells them that, if their ICP and yours are the same, they should have success growing their customer lifetime value by adding your product to their suite. To investors, growth indicates that you have a business that has potential and merits an increase in valuation. This driver is primarily impacted by Sales and Marketing, but revenue to existing customers is often influenced by new features delivered by Engineering. Ideally, you have a mix of customer number growth and customer revenue growth.

MARGIN

Margin is defined generally as the amount your company retains from customer sales after paying for the costs associated with that sale. In other words, if your margin is low, it may indicate that your growth is being done inefficiently. If it is high, it may indicate that you can continue to grow in a capital-efficient way. Capital efficiency is particularly important in demonstrating to investors that your growth is sustainable. This indicator is most heavily impacted, and improved, during the Standardization and Optimization phases, as that is when you squeeze out costs and inefficiencies in your operations. This driver is primarily impacted by Shared Services and their ability to create efficient processes throughout your company. Ideally, you monitor both your gross margins (what you keep after cost of sales) and net margins (what you keep after paying for costs *not* directly attached to a sale) to ensure your growth is manageable and scalable.

RETENTION

Retention is defined as the percent of acquired customers you keep, as well as their revenue over time. If customer or revenue retention is low, it likely indicates a lack of product-market fit or issues in customer success and onboarding. If customer or revenue retention is high, it likely indicates you are on the right track, as customers stay or come back for more.

Retention is the single most valuable metric you can look at, because it always tells the truth. Anyone can be sold to once, or given discounts to sign on the dotted line, but if they aren't happy and stop using the product, they will not stick around. If retention trends are negative, this is one of the most likely reasons a deal will fail to close. This driver is impacted by everyone in your company—from Sales signing up customers that are not aligned with your agreed ICP, to products that fail to meet the needs expressed by customer requests, sales, and services. It crafts your future road map. Ideally, customer and revenue retention are both above 90 percent over the long term, which indicates strong product-market fit and a sustainable business.

Valuation Drivers—A Closer Look

While most agree that determining valuations is as much an art as it is a science, it's important to look at value as *subjective*, as it can mean different things to different startups and investors. What you're really after here is the multiples of value your startup can achieve. The primary purpose is to determine multiples, which are often determined via a comparative analysis that evaluates similar startups using standardized financial metrics.

The market will then review where your startup sits within the ecosystem and assign a specific value based on many of the factors you've identified in your ecosystem. Your ability to understand your startup's valuation factors and present them alongside your vision during due diligence will dictate what valuation your startup can command.

Let's now walk through some of the most critical valuation drivers one by one and find out how to best prepare for the due diligence your potential acquirer might conduct.

Revenue growth is one of the most common factors that drives startups toward strategic exits. It is also the factor you have the most control over.

In order to understand a startup's growth potential, an acquirer or investor will focus their diligence on historical trend reporting, where they will dig in on positive or negative spikes and address them with the founder and their team to understand what triggered the spike and how the team executed against it. This allows the investor or acquirer to understand the strength of the team in forecasting the startup, as well as pivoting to address current and future needs. When it comes to due diligence regarding revenue growth, I typically review the following aspects:

- **Pricing Power:** Does the startup understand how their current prices compare to potential future prices they may charge for new products or services? How has the ideal customer profile responded to pricing changes and discount incentives in the past?

- **New Logo Growth:** What is the concentration of revenue and what is the startup's ability to acquire net new clients? Are existing customers "tapped out" in terms of revenue growth, or is there still significant runway?

- **Churn Rate:** Are existing customers not only staying with the product, but spending more as time progresses?

- **Market and Competitor Growth Rate:** The mark of a great startup is one that grows faster than the market and its competitors. For example, if industry growth is 10 percent annually, and you are growing at 20 percent annually, that indicates that you are taking more than your proportional share of an industry's growth.

- **Customer and Revenue Concentration:** The 80/20 rule applies here. Does 80 percent of your revenue come from 20 percent of your customers? If so, how have you protected your vulnerability with your contracts and go-to-market strategy? In other words, if your top five customers left tomorrow, could you survive and thrive? This is a big issue when you look to exit. Your buyer will look at revenue concentration as risk; this is because you simply have too many eggs in a single basket. Concentration is why you separate revenue from customer retention, growth, and margin. The concentration of these things will often be intertangled and thus present risk across the board. Lose that big customer, and you still have more people, office space, and other expenses you must contend with, not to mention the fact that you now have to rebuild that revenue. This can be a huge issue. It feels good to land a whale, but to be safe, every whale must be offset by dolphins.

- **Geographic Concentration:** Are all of your customers in a country that I also operate in? Is there geopolitical risk in your customer base?

- **Time Until Revenue:** Are your customers generating revenue quickly? Or are implementation times long and arduous? Are you collecting on that revenue easily and in a timely manner? Or do you have to send customers to collections?

Margins are often overlooked in a strategic exit. Why? Most acquirers have the resources to significantly improve the margins on your product or service by absorbing your smaller operations into their much-larger, well-oiled machine. For this reason, *operating* margins can be under-weighted by many founders in the pursuit of growth. However, gross margins remain important to acquirers because they indicate that the product itself and the cost of providing that product are within their parameters.

If during your valuation driver analysis, you determine margin is a priority for your acquirers, here are several things an acquirer will consider and investigate in their diligence:

- **Staff:** Is the current staff skilled enough to increase productivity and sales without increasing overhead expenses? Are they running their functional areas with optimal efficiency or is there room to improve?

- **Vendor Expenses:** Typically, as a startup grows, they're able to secure lower costs through volume discounts. SaaS startups typically incur high hosting expenses to start. Is revenue increasing at a faster rate than expenses? If you are a tech to tech-enabled service, then you must separate the costs of innovation and research and development (R&D) from maintenance. There are two reasons for this. First is that an investor or acquirer can see where you are with the product by simply looking at how much of your product and engineering budget is spent on innovation and R&D. This may indicate that the product is still under development and maintenance, which shows how well the technology scales up. Let's say you are looking to buy a house. There are the costs of the house, there could be a cost of the kitchen remodel, and then there are the costs of utilities. You want to be able to show that maintenance is low and the product is complete. Yes, I know, no product is ever complete, but it should not cost the same when you are building as it does when you are in the Optimization phase. Optimization is everywhere, across all functional areas. I can tell you that, when you do this in technology, you will have the biggest pushback of any functional area, and I can tell you it's one worth the confrontation.

- **Margin Benefits:** Can you save money for the acquirer by adding efficiencies, tools, software automation, and so on?

- **Efficient Scalability:** If the acquirer rolled your product out across their entire customer base tomorrow, could they do so in a cost-effective way?

- **Market Penetration:** The acquirer will want to know whether you have only captured the low-hanging fruit or whether your product is strong enough to capture more difficult customers. Have you left them some runway, or is it all uphill for the acquirer post-acquisition with high customer acquisition costs?

If only a few percentage points change in gross margins, it can materially affect a valuation, so it's critically important to understand revenues and cost of goods sold, how they scale as a startup grows, and how they can impact your bottom line. Sometimes an acquirer will purchase a startup that will become a product line of a larger company, where margins can be improved through centralized resources, or synergies. Sometimes they will continue to run the startup independently, and margins matter a great deal. Understanding your ideal acquirer profile is vital in determining whether margin valuation drivers will matter to a potential acquirer.

Valuation Drivers
Measured within your ICP

GROWTH
- Recurring increase in customers & revenue
- Indicates in-ICP customers are willing to pay for your product

MARGIN
- The revenue retained from a sale, after paying the costs associated with that sale
- Low margin → ineffecient growth

RETENTION
- The percent of acquired customers & revenue you keep over a period of time
- Low retention → product market misalignment or poor customer support

Using Your Key Performance Indicators

Much earlier, we mentioned that key performance indicators (KPIs) would play an important role in your startup reaching the final phase. Now it's time to take a closer look at KPIs.

Typically, there are two distinct types of KPIs—leading and lagging. Leading KPIs are things to be done in the future, while lagging KPIs are what has been done already.

- Leading KPIs are precursors of future financial success and move lagging indicators, so think of them as the future.
- Lagging indicators show how successful the organization was at achieving results in the past and moved valuation drivers.

Let's walk through an example of leading and lagging indicators in practice. In the below example, you can see the KPI waterfall playing out as follows:

Our valuation driver here is growth, which is driven primarily by Sales and Marketing, with some influence by Product and Engineering.

In the context of marketing, if Marketing is failing to produce enough content to reach your ideal customer profile (ICP) and marketing qualified lead (MQL) targets in the beginning of the quarter (leading), it is virtually impossible that they will achieve their MQL goals by the end of the quarter, which means you are looking at a lagging indicator.

Understanding leading and lagging indicator connections allows you to intervene in real time, as soon as a leading KPI indicates a functional area or employee will not achieve their lagging KPI. Instead of waiting until the end of the quarter to speak with your team, if any single team member misses their leading KPI, you know it warrants a point Kaizen conversation in real time. If you do this, you can effect change quickly before the financial close.

KPI performance reporting must always be done in the context of what we refer to as "plan, actual, and difference." While simple, this means you are constantly presenting your current plan against the current actual data, with the difference displayed in black and white. This can often be intimidating to teams as they (correctly) understand that there is nowhere to hide anymore. That said, if you create a progressive culture, they will appreciate them. It's a lot harder to have a bad quarter and not know it's coming when your leading indicators have been off plan. Leading and lagging indicators, paired with plan, actual, and difference reporting, are invaluable tools in creating a high performing organization.

StartupScience.io breaks KPIs down by functional area, category (relating to income or expense), and type (leading and lagging). While each functional area is monitoring their own leading/lagging indicators, leadership is reviewing both their KPI "stack" from the top down, as well as each functional area's KPI from the bottom up.

In the next section, we'll walk through each functional area's KPI stack with suggestions on implementation. Each of these stacks ultimately rolls up to the C-suite's management stack that exposes the performance of the entire startup.

The Key Performance Indicator Stack

A KPI stack refers to a set of KPIs that are utilized collectively to measure and assess your performance as a business or the performance of a specific department. And while every KPI we've included has a specific role and function, each typically maps one of the broader startup goals we advise you to focus on: growth (more customers, more revenue), margin (greater operating or gross profits), and retention (low or negative churn).

Regardless of your startup's industry, size, or revenue, the logic is always the same: leading KPIs drive lagging KPIs, which, in turn, drives your valuation. We have resources to map the stack for each functional area. Below is a sample.

Content leads to marketing qualified lead (MQL) engagement, MQL engagement leads to sales-qualified leads (SQLs), SQLs lead to demos, demos lead to contracts, contracts lead to new customers, and new customers lead to growth. Then look at customer satisfaction measured by Net Promoter Scores, which is a leading indicator of customer retention. Tracking plan and actual tells you which KPIs are on target and which need work.

The KPI Stack

KPI	LEAD/LAG	FINANCIAL	VALUATION DRIVER	PLAN	ACTUAL	BETTER/ WORSE
Revenue Growth $ Annually recurring income	Lag	Income	Growth	$100,000	$125,000	
Demos Completed	Lead	Expense	Growth	45	78	
Gross Margin	Lag	Expense	Margin	80%	75%	
Contact to Contract Days in sales pipeline	Lead	Expense	Margin	60	85	
Customer Retention	Lag	Income	Retention	350	325	
NPS	Lead	Income	Retention	65	45	

Once you have your KPI stack and best practices in place, you can go to work on optimization, and the financial math behind optimization, some of which is easy. Some not so much.

Focus on the Cost of the Action, Optimizing, and Measuring

In this example, one way to focus on the cost of the action is to optimize and measure the cost benefit in terms of payroll. There are countless other business cycles that could also be analyzed and measured, such as contract to revenue, new employees' cycle-time from day one to reaching 100 percent productivity, and literally anything in your KPI stack. The process of optimization can cause anxiety for teams if done incorrectly, scaring them into thinking you're eliminating their jobs; however, there is a right way that does not create such emotion.

I like to think of this as the process of really allowing your people to express their ideas for better ways of doing things. I can tell you that this approach has not once backfired. Most people want to tell you better ways of doing things, without needing any prodding on your part. They want to tell you what frustrates them and what drives them crazy. Think of this process the same way you think about customer feedback. It must be offered, and it must be heard and absorbed. If you do not act on it, there's a strong likelihood it will happen again, and even worse, they will just stop providing it! We have all heard the watercooler talk: "I told them, and as usual, nothing happened." Remember this process because it's the key to optimization.

The Good News and the Bad News

Okay, so how do you actually gather employee feedback? Well, the good news is, it's easy to explain. But the bad news is, it takes dedicated time from important people and your functional area leaders.

- **Step One:** I always have a functional area leader review the KPIs, which will reveal areas to focus upon. I also want them to review the best practices within the folder structure and make notes on areas in which they have questions.
- **Step Two:** The functional area leader should make an appointment with the department head and a couple of the highest performers to walk through the best practices on-screen and show the job being done, called "shadowing." It's important to note that just having them walk through the best practices will not result in what you're after. You're simply showing the areas from which you hope to elicit employee feedback.

Most often what you are after is found in the conversations that take place between the planned meetings, such as during breaks, when people make quick mentions of issues that bother them. You'll hear things like, "OMG, that drives me crazy," or "I swear I'm always waiting for this stupid thing to work," and so on. This is where you get the real feedback . . . from people talking.

Listen and make a note of any place that requires a change of focus. Most common are moving from software application to software application, opening sheets, opening docs, trying to find things in your folder structure, searching for things, asking people questions, waiting on people's answers . . . you get the idea. What you are looking for at first is how you can keep them focused and in their swim lane, and how you can prevent frustration, confusion, and disruption to others. Look for patterns—where people are saying the same thing. Of course, once you've heard the feedback and understand the problems, it's up to your functional leaders and their teams to make adjustments.

Now that you have the steps to optimization, wash, rinse, and repeat every year, and you will find many other benefits. For instance, your functional area leaders will be in lockstep with their areas (which is rare), you will have a unified culture that embraces change, and you will have a seamless process. As customers go through your company, you will find that your margins grow, and your valuation drivers reach new heights. This is perhaps the most obvious benefit outside financial. Your people will be much happier, and you will hold on to them. In my studies on this subject, I found, surprisingly, that pay was not the most important thing. Good people rank happiness above pay every time so long as they are getting paid in the market. Good people want to contribute, and many will leave if they don't feel that they are contributing.

Building the Foundation for Growth

In the next chapter, we talk about growth. This phase follows Standardization and Optimization because hitting a growth stride before you lock down your operations will only exaggerate the issues that you should have cleaned up with those two phases.

What you are doing is building the foundation required to handle the weight that growth will place on your operations and every single functional area. In my interviews with fighter pilots, I talked to one pilot who told me a story about an elite group of pilots testing some jets. During this process, they found, when they were done, they were all *sick* . . . every time. After months and extensive testing of virtually everything, right before they were out of options, they found a tiny part that costs around sixty cents was the problem. This was a multibillion-dollar aircraft being flown by some of the best pilots in the world, and a sixty-cent part created a massive disruption. The point is, you are only as strong as your weakest link, regardless of the size or price, and the weakest link *will*, without fail, be the thing that creates the biggest problems. Find them early, test the tensile strength of your startup before you depend on it, remember my story of El Capitan, and pull the rope before you depend on it!

Earlier on, I mentioned my training for a marathon swim and how my Apple Watch was helping me keep track of my progress through KPIs. During this training, I spent hundreds of hours refining every detail— breathing, kicking, the arm stroke, the hand position, the hip rotation, the head position—all to create a flow to move my body through the water as frictionlessly as possible, with the least energy and the most power. If I did any of these things wrong, I used more energy, and moved slower. And in a marathon swim, you need to conserve energy.

I mention the marathon swimming analogy because I often think about how important it is to eliminate friction when starting up and running your business. I recommend that you move the startup to the Startup Science Lifecycle as fast as possible, with the least costs and the most power. The optimization process is, to me, the same thing. Before you bring your startup into the race, you must be as frictionless as possible, with the least energy and the most power.

I have a startup in my portfolio that is in this situation. The startup moved into the Growth phase very quickly, only to discover they didn't have the head count to handle customers, which then turned into a "yard sale." The issue was found in a disorganized organization chart, resulting in them barely hanging on, despite the CEO and team working all hours just to maintain the startup. They are now working through the Standardization and Optimization phases, but it's slow and painful and is now slowing sales. In their case, slowing sales meant giving the team some air cover so they could get ready for the growth. In their words to me, "God, I hope people read that book. It would have changed my miserable life right now."

I'll leave you with this: under pressure, a business will show its leaks, but at the most inconvenient time. Remember the fire roads used by firemen fighting wildfires? Do all of the important things in advance, even the smallest things, so you don't have to contend with the big "fires"!

CHAPTER WRAP-UP

After completing a series of optimizations, you've made some meaningful improvements to your startup. These improvements include establishing a culture of Kaizen (point and systematic). You've simplified best practices, and you're seeing measured increases in growth, margin, and retention. Your KPIs have become actionable as part of your value-capturing machine. And for every dollar put into your well-oiled machine, you're generating a higher return and burning less cash along the way. Now you are ready to fund and launch your Growth phase. Remember that spending on growth before optimization leads to fires and weaker profit margins. If you are interested in how to get more tactical, watch, listen, read, and experience courses can be found by scanning this QR code. You will also find best practices, templates, examples, and suggested software (incentives offered by the providers) and how to get them.

Phase Six: Growth

Companies that grow for the sake of growth or that expand into areas outside of their core business strategy, often stumble. On the other hand, companies that build scale for the benefit of their customers and shareholders more often succeed over time.

—Jamie Dimon, Chairman of the Board and Chief Executive Officer of JPMorgan Chase & Co.

In one of my annual adventures, I decided to drive an actual NASCAR car at Pikes Peak International Raceway, which, at the time, was the fastest one-mile, paved oval anywhere in the world. After climbing through the car window, I fired up the 500+ horsepower engine that sounded like thunder and sent shivers down my spine.

I hit the accelerator for fifty adrenaline-filled laps at one of the most challenging raceways. In seconds, I was hauling ass, as I saw in front of me a steep thirty-plus-degree bend, which looked like a wall . . . and I mean, an actual wall! I was coached by my guide to "keep up the speed." I felt as though I was seconds away from hitting this straight on. At that precise moment, the car hit the bend and whipped around the turn, sticking to the track like glue, and as it did, my body snapped to the side with the belts, which were the only thing holding me in place. I stayed focused as the car completed the turn, and I saw the upcoming straightaway, at which point my guide told me to "hit the gas *hard*." The car whipped a bit, and straightened as I shot down the straightaway.

So, what does my adrenaline-chasing drive have to do with growth and scale? Well, NASCAR tracks are banked at various degrees to create greater momentum and velocity through the turns. The angle of the track directs the rest of the force toward the center, the direction the driver is trying to turn. The extra force from the banked track, combined with the friction from the tires, is enough to turn the car safely.

As a startup enters the Growth and Scale phase of the Startup Science Lifecycle, it must have momentum, which is simply the strength it gains when it is growing. This allows the startup to continue to grow stronger and/or faster as time passes, exiting each curve faster than it entered.

Good Growth / Bad Growth

While it may seem counterintuitive, not all growth for a startup is necessarily good. An exceedingly broad customer base can be very costly to service. And if your goal is to sell your startup, customer growth not aligned with your potential acquirer's customer base is wasted effort! I learned that lesson the hard way.

Back when I was building Affiliate Traction—I was about five years in, and I thought I was doing a great job. My customers were paying real money for our products and services, my investors were happy, and I'd gotten deep into acquisition talks with a deep-pocketed company. On paper, Affiliate Traction was worth many millions. It looked like, pretty soon, I was going to be rich.

When the acquirer I had been cultivating took a closer look at Affiliate Traction, they realized that about half our startup customers came from lead generation rather than retail, and that didn't align with their own business model. "We're only interested in people who are buying products," my contact told me. "We won't pay for the rest. And we don't want the hassle of taking them over, so you'll need to get rid of them before we can make a deal."

Bad growth is also growth made for the sake of growing. Companies expand businesses, staff, and other areas in an attempt to seduce investors and make a splash in the media. The problem is that, with so much data readily available, the smart investors today can see the bottom line, and recognize when a business is not benefiting from more people or larger offices.

The Difference Between Scale and Growth

Growth is a familiar term in business and elsewhere. When we think of something *increasing* we think of growth. The problem is that growth and scale are often used interchangeably and, therefore, incorrectly. They are also often regarded with a degree of enthusiasm that does not properly convey the high level of risk present in the Growth phase. In reality, growth is one of the driver valuations of scaling your startup. Scaling a business is about increasing revenues through various factors that include growth, as well as gross margin and retention of customers.

Scaling and Economies of Scale

Startup *growth* is about increasing top-line revenues, often at any cost, whereas *scaling* a startup is about increasing revenues, while effectively improving your profit margin and retaining your customers. Economists refer to this as "economies of scale."

If you make widgets for $5 and sell them for $8, and both parts of that equation are inflexible, your startup can grow but not scale, because your costs will rise at the same rate as your revenues and profits. If, however, you can reduce your costs, perhaps by way of a volume discount from a supplier, or as we discussed earlier, by optimizing through best practices, you might be able to scale your startup and earn higher profits. Often, the human mind thinks of *growth* in linear terms: a startup adds new resources (capital, people, or technology). You can actually see the company growing. By contrast, *scaling* does not necessarily increase size of staff, number of products, or anything tangible other than revenue. One thing that drives me nuts is people using the number of employees to judge size. This is full of flawed assumptions. Size is not about how many people you have working for you. Size should be based on customers (revenue), not employees (costs), and any measure by employee should be evaluated after growth, margin, and retention evaluation.

Processes that scale are those that can be done en masse without extra effort. If I send an email to ten people or one million, my effort is essentially the same. This concept is particularly important for technology-related startups that are often zero-marginal cost startup models, which allow very effective scaling once prior phases are completed.

Investors and would-be acquirers look for economies of scale, which means your gross margin should grow over time. Growth must happen before you can scale your startup, but your ability to scale is often a constraining factor on your growth. It's a bit like driving in traffic. You can't just hit the gas pedal. Instead, you need to ensure you're driving safely at your current speed, and then accelerate at a safe, sustainable pace. You also need to keep an eye on what's in front of you, which can block your progress. That doesn't mean going slow. It just means not going too fast, too soon. Without growth, you won't achieve scale or find your way to an exit. But grow too fast, and you'll run out of steam and slide back down again. It's by balancing the two, and growing no faster than you're able to scale, that you can unlock your startup's full potential.

The NASCAR guide (who was a real character, by the way) explained to me "power-to-weight" ratio, which is a measurement of actual performance of any engine or power source.

Power-to-Weight Ratio

The power-to-weight ratio simply dictates how much power you need to move—more weight, more power. This might sound obvious, but it's something that trips up a lot of founders, not least because investors are usually pushing them to grow as fast as possible, which takes us back to the trouble with Silicon Valley, as we discussed earlier. The entire process of planning and validating your startup is like drawing up the blueprints for a machine that turns one dollar into two dollars. Convince investors that your machine works, and they'll want to feed as many dollars in as possible, and as quickly as possible.

The Goal Is a Controlled Burn

The problem is that the machine you've built is really an assembly line. Sure, you want the conveyor belt to move as fast as possible, but right at the end of the conveyor belt sits your service, and other retention functions. Start plowing products through the production line too quickly, and you'll wind up overloading your retention capabilities, and everything will spill out all over the floor. Worse still, if you spent all your money on the sales and marketing functions that come earlier in the process, you might not have the resources to scale up your retention function. Again, you will have started to grow too fast, too soon.

Instead of front-loading everything by focusing purely on rapid growth, you need to be prepared to buck your investors and slow things down in the name of sustainable success. The goal isn't a runaway wildfire; it's a controlled burn that lets you manage your startup's growth and achieve more in the long run.

Back when I begged and pleaded for an opportunity to prove myself as a wholesale lender, I was given a pretty rough area of Los Angeles, only because nobody else wanted it. One day, the CEO of the bank I had begged to work for (who took an interest in me and became like a father to me) called me into the office. We then jumped into his car, and he took me to a bus stop and told me to get out and wait on the bus bench in the summer heat in East LA (no, not for the bus).

This went on for months, and every week I would sit there for about an hour. He would come back after lunch, pick me up, hand me a sandwich, and ask me what I learned. Hot, frustrated, and slightly embarrassed, I said, "Well, I saw a sign in the lot across the road that said 'Coming Soon.' Then, as things progressed, I saw fences, and then electrical poles, and then the building went up quickly."

Then he asked me, "What did you learn about that process?"

I explained that, once the foundation was done, things went pretty fast.

He slapped my shoulder and said, "That's right. Planning and setting a strong foundation are the keys to success. If you don't do it right, the building will fall under its own weight."

In that sense, launching a startup *isn't* a haphazard endeavor to flip for quick profits. It's more like constructing a building. Sure, you could just focus on building your structure taller and taller, but sooner or later, the whole edifice will sway, wobble, then collapse. Instead of just facing forward and building something tall, you also need to slow things down and build a solid structure *beneath* you so that every new layer rests on a solid foundation.

That's where the process of using KPIs and best practices to standardize your operations comes into play. If everyone on your team is choosing their own adventure, you'll soon find that your customer retention suffers. If people have different experiences each time they do business with you (some good, some bad), they probably will find a competitor who offers greater consistency.

In most cases, whether you're a software firm or pharmacy, if retention fails, you are sliding down a very, very slippery slope. We term this a "cleanup" or "turnaround." That's how common it is. There are even specialists, like me and others, who do this full-time. Climbing out of such a predicament costs more time, money, and people than most companies can handle. Only by putting best practices in place can you ensure consistent experiences for your customers and put the foundations and support structures in place that will enable you to deliver truly scalable success.

Identifying Your Scaling-Specific KPI and Exit Requirements

In Phase Five (Optimization), you spent a significant amount of time implementing KPI stacks for each functional area, as well as for the

C-suite. In addition, you linked your KPIs to your valuation drivers, such that the entire startup is now aligned around the KPI and valuation drivers that target your ideal acquirer profile. Now that you've identified *all* of the KPI valuation drivers that are relevant for your startup, you need to identify the *subset* that is relevant for scaling your startup.

Not every KPI is necessarily *scaling-specific.* A scaling-specific KPI is one that specifically allows you to understand whether you are scaling your startup effectively, or, from our prior section, growing your startup without adding proportionate costs to obtain that growth. KPIs are heavily dependent on the aspects of your startup that you need to scale, in order to reach your valuation drivers and ideal acquirer profile's exit requirements.

Let's walk through an example of how to identify your scaling-specific KPIs and link them to your valuation drivers.

Everyone likes ice cream, so let's try to scale my ice cream parlor, Greg's Frozen Delights, which is located in an up-and-coming restaurant district and produces ten homemade flavors to sell to walk-up customers every day. The ideal acquirer profile (IAP) has three requirements (valuation drivers): that our sales must be greater than $2M per month, that we have at least twenty taste-tested and approved flavors on our menu, and that each flavor has sales of at least $50,000 per month. Greg's Frozen Delights is currently making around $45,000 per flavor, per month, netting $450,000 in total sales.

In this example, our core mission is to scale-specific KPIs, which are the number of flavor choices (going from ten to twenty), sales per flavor (going from $45,000 to at least $50,000 for existing flavors and $0 to at least $50,000 for new flavors), and overall sales (going from $0.5M per month to $2M per month). You'll notice that each mission and objective has a scaling-specific KPI directly *linked* to a valuation driver. You'll also likely have noticed that, while these are the headline KPIs, these are *lagging* indicators, as they are all currency KPIs, which means they'll only tell us whether we're hitting our goals *after* time has passed.

This would call for a mission to go from $450,000 in total sales to $2M per month. The objectives are the steps to accomplish this, starting at the beginning with marketing content and other activities, and flowing down to sales leads, sales demos, contracts, and so on.

In order to be successful, we need to ensure that we've attached *leading* indicators to our lagging, scaling-specific KPIs. For example, historically, Greg's Frozen Delights has had to test five new flavors to ultimately find one that will net close to our target sales threshold. We can also only test two new flavors per month to ensure we don't turn away customers looking for their favorites. We wouldn't want our customers to "churn." Therefore, if we want to sell Greg's Frozen Delights in one year, that means we need to test fifty new flavors in total, and at a rate of two per month, which would mean it will take us twenty-five months to test and find all of our new flavors. This is much longer than our target exit time frame, which tells us we need to either adjust our exit time frame expectation or add flavor-testing capability as a scaling-specific KPI to improve upon. This means our leading indicator to achieving enough successful flavors is that we are testing enough flavors per month (five) in order to sell the startup in a year, which may mean we need to open another location (grow the business) or host testing sessions to speed up the process.

As you can see, every scaling-specific KPI should be linked to both a leading indicator, as well as an ideal acquirer profile exit requirement. These links ensure you are scaling *for a reason*, not just because your executive team *feels* like it, or your investors *feel* like it is the right thing to do. I've seen far too many founders scale without being thoughtful about how and where their scaling will lead their startup. Ensuring that each of your scaling-specific KPIs is linked to a leading indicator and an ideal acquirer profile exit requirement all but guarantees you'll scale in a thoughtful manner.

Allocating Resources to Scale Your Startup

While we've identified our scaling-specific KPIs and linked them to their leading indicators and exit criteria, we now need to realign each functional area to achieve our goals. The best practices you created in Phase Four (Standardization) and optimized and refined in Phase Five (Optimization) are crucial here.

For example, if we need to scale our flavor-testing operations by opening a new store, Marketing needs to build a launch plan, Finance needs to adjust our accounting policies, Legal needs to obtain permits or agreements, and most importantly, Operations needs to find a way to potentially double their production of ice cream.

If we go with the tasting sessions, we'll need Marketing to use social media to convince existing or new customers to attend the ice cream tasting sessions. Customer Service will have to add staff to serve those customers, Legal will need to create waivers, Finance will need to arrange ticket sales, and yet again, Operations will need to create more ice cream!

Any direction you choose to take will need to refer back to each functional area's KPI stack to ensure that their part of the puzzle has leading and lagging indicators attached for proper monitoring against your overall plan. For example, if Operations needs to double their output, and they can produce one flavor per machine, we either need to figure out a way to produce more flavors per machine or we may need to double the number of machines we own. In either case, Operations has specific, tangible next steps they need to achieve against the overall goals of the startup.

Each of these examples also illustrates the degree of effort required by just one exit criteria. If our exit timeline is one year, that means we likely needed to start aligning our functional areas yesterday! But having Greg's Frozen Delights' executive team realize this alignment issue now, one year before we want to sell, is significantly better than realizing it three *months* prior to our target sell date. At this phase (Growth), we still have time to adjust the entire operation to better scale toward our ideal acquirer profile's requirements.

If you think all the way back to Phase One (Vision), this is why we asked you to better understand your ideal acquirer profiles and exit criteria at the very beginning. While you can always adjust in Phase Six (Growth), it will cost you much more time and effort than being aligned with your ideal acquirer profile exit criteria from the start. It all goes back to building the foundation. It's easier, cheaper, and less risky to build a foundation before you build the house than it is to try strengthening the foundation of the house later.

Optimizing How You Scale

About three months after Greg's Frozen Delights started conducting flavor-testing sessions, a clever operations manager realized that we could double the number of flavors that would ultimately succeed due to the faster accumulation of tasting data. This meant that, instead of identifying three flavors per month, we could identify *six* successful flavors per month via the tasting sessions. Finally, a bit of luck! This meant that our exit timeline of one year was now back on track *in terms of identifying flavors*. But what about ensuring we would achieve our overall revenue goal as well?

While we may believe we are on track to achieve *one* of our ideal acquirer profile's exit criteria, we've now realized that we need to optimize the remainder of our operations to successfully *sell* all of those new flavors. After all, *having* new flavors is only part of the plan. The other key part is *selling* more ice cream to increase revenue. For example, at Greg's Frozen Delights, this may mean understanding more precisely, down to the ingredient-sourcing level, what is necessary for each flavor to achieve at least $50,000 in sales, while focusing on our most popular flavors to bring in a multiple of our ideal acquirer's flavor minimum. Additionally, whereas before Greg's Frozen Delights might have been able to get away with being understaffed at times, we may want to *overstaff* now to ensure that we serve every customer, even at the expense of profitability (you'll note that our ideal acquirer profile did not mention profitability, only revenue).

This is now the exact moment where many startups raise "growth rounds" to double down on their scaling-specific KPIs and accelerate the rate at which they progress toward their exit. They should really be called "scale rounds," but we must admit, "growth" sounds sexier. But you know better! We don't want to just mindlessly grow at this point. We want to scale, and move the startup toward our ideal acquirer profile exit criteria.

At this point, you should continually be evaluating which parts of your startup can effectively handle more fuel, whatever that may be, to accelerate your progress toward your ideal acquirer profile exit criteria, like the NASCAR, after the turn when I hit the accelerator and it took off down the straightaway. If you've noticed that you can put $10 into operations and churn out $20, you should invest those dollars until a different part of your startup offers you a better return for your scaling dollars. It is in this phase that you are laser-focused on ensuring your scaling-specific KPI indicates that you are well funded, so you can concentrate all of the momentum of the startup on the areas your ideal acquirer profile values most. Phase Seven (Exit) will capitalize on these efforts as you drive toward your ultimate exit.

CHAPTER WRAP-UP

At this point, you are continuing to improve your best practices as your startup scales. Your scaling-specific KPI is linked to leading indicators and exit criteria, and the startup is running like a well-oiled machine. You're growing at a rate that is somewhere between comfortable and uncomfortable. You're also likely in a position to raise your next round, if needed, and prepare for your exit. It's likely been six to twelve months since you've completed Phase 4 (Standardization).

Phase Seven: Exit

Give me six hours to chop down a tree and I will spend
the first four sharpening the ax.

—Unknown

When you start out with clear eyes, realistic goals, and define success down to realistic levels, you don't just minimize your chance of failure; you also establish a shorter timeline for success. If you play your cards right, you'll be able to complete your first exit and build another successful startup, and then another one, while your unicorn-obsessed peers are still struggling with their first startup.

It's important that you don't get tripped up by your own ambitions. Instead, take a more sober approach and focus on building a startup that has a realistic shot at success. It might not be quite as exciting as claiming that you're building the next Facebook or Google, but starting a business or getting into several startups should not be an ego trip. Do the smart thing: put your ego on hold, lower your sights a little, and stay focused on building a startup that actually has a shot at success. Remember, success doesn't mean popularity and media hype. It means more than enough money to change your life and that of your family . . . and extended family. There are many successful exits of highly profitable startups that aren't nearly as well known and talked about as Google or Meta, but they provided their founders with amazing results.

For tech startups, that means moving from vision to acquisition in *just five years*. Aim for less than that, and you'll run too hot and likely wind up selling before the optimum time. Go longer, and you'll wind up losing your seat at the table (remember, musical chairs) before you're able to secure a suitable exit.

During that period, stay laser-focused on efficiently building a startup that is designed to attract investors and position you for a solid exit on a timetable that works for you. This might sound a bit calculating, but to win, it's essential to understand that, for most startups, the best possible outcome isn't a multibillion-dollar IPO, it's a well-timed, clean, high-valuation exit that returns two to five times for your investors.

The key insight that most investors have, and that most new founders lack, is that every startup is born, grows, and matures in a predictable way. In other words, every startup follows the same basic lifecycle: from vision through pre-seed fundraising, then on to seed rounds and growth series A round, series B round, and so on. At each phase of the process, there's a different goal—from working through your "proof of concept" to developing a product, to validating your product, establishing a customer base, going to market, growing the business, and then to go on to an acquisition. This is why the first conversation we have with every founder is to make sure they understand the Startup Science Lifecycle.

Finding the Right Buyer

In any acquisition, you'll find that your buyer places a premium on some parts of your startup, and discounts others. To get the exit you are seeking, you need to invest your time and energy in developing the parts of your startup that will generate market value when the time comes to sell—and that means creating the maximum possible alignment between your startup and the needs of your acquirer.

The key to developing that alignment is to start out with a clear sense, not just of what you're building, but of who you're building it for. Just as you once validated your product by figuring out whether it met the actual needs of your ideal customers, you need to ensure that your startup meets the needs of your *acquirer*. Get that wrong, and things won't go well. It doesn't matter how great your startup is. If it isn't the *right* startup for your target acquirer, the deal is never going to happen.

As mentioned in the early part of the book, as a founder, you *should* start thinking about your exit years earlier, when you are first launching your startup. The Startup Science Lifecycle is designed, in large part, to help you achieve that. This is precisely why we recommend identifying your ideal acquirer profile while you are fleshing out your vision's North Star.

Once you've identified your ideal acquirer profile, you'll need to introduce yourself to them, and start the discussion that will one day lead to a deal. It's important to start this early on, before you've locked your startup into a path that diverges from the needs of your acquirer. Many founders worry about this, and think they'll be laughed out of the room if they contact their ideal acquirers before they've proven the value of their startup. The reality is that these are conversations that corporations *want* to be having, especially with early-phase startups. It's so important that most major corporations have their own accelerator programs to stay in the know on future acquisitions.

Like I said early in the book, the large enterprise businesses don't *build* innovation, they *buy* it. Your business *is* their innovation, so don't be shy. It's in their interest for you to build a startup that's a value advisory board to them, so you'll usually get a warm reception if you can move past your anxiety and simply pick up the phone and ask to speak with someone in Corporate Development. Typically, Corporate Development is responsible for increasing revenues through growth, which includes building strategic partnerships, as well as expansion and acquisitions. If your business aligns closely with the needs of the company, they will likely want to speak with you about your startup. Of course, you need to be ready to present your startup in the best light.

Ecosystem Alignment

By definition, your ideal acquirer profile will be a business with the means to purchase a growing startup. More now than ever, such businesses have clear processes in place to manage potential acquisitions, and also have people who are tasked with sourcing deals. These people are always eager to chat with up-and-coming founders and will be happy to tell you about their process, their criteria for assessing startups, and the kinds of startups they're looking to acquire.

Often, you'll find your contacts can spell out in very clear terms what they're looking for from potential acquisitions. You might find, for instance, that a potential buyer only thinks seriously about buying startups that have $2.5M in annual recurring revenue (ARR). That sort of clear benchmark is extremely useful, because it tells you exactly where you need to be in order to move the process forward. By checking off the various other requirements that your acquirer has articulated—from ideal customer profile, to technical integration, to co-marketing—you can work toward a point where securing an acquisition delivers clear value for both sides.

The trick, as you start to have these conversations, is to figure out how much authority the person you're talking to actually has. Often, it's useful simply to ask the person you're talking to what their role is: Are they simply scouting around for potential acquisitions, or are they involved in actively vetting and approving deals? You'll need to climb the food chain as quickly as you can (but on pace with your current startup phase), and build relationships with people who have the authority to approve a deal or the institutional clout needed to effectively champion your startup to higher-ups in their organization.

As you build deeper relationships with increasingly influential partners, you'll gain a deeper understanding of what your acquirer is looking for. If they're seeking your technology, you'll need to make sure they have chemistry with your head of technology. If they're mostly trying to drive growth, your revenue officer or the head of your customer success team might be much more important. By cultivating these relationships and showing that you're willing to listen and accommodate your startup to deliver value for the acquirer, you'll be able to turn your contacts into champions for your startup, and to sow the seeds of a successful exit.

The Three Points of Acquirer Validation

The acquirer is essentially looking for synergies between your startup and their company to ensure that there are additional opportunities to capitalize on the investment in the future.

Here are some important considerations to review, as you look at potential synergies:

- **Customer:** Can the acquirer sell their products to my customers and vice versa? Are there areas to reduce combined sales and marketing efforts required to win a new customer? Does the customer's lifetime value increase? The trick is finding the opportunities to maximize the combination of products and customer bases. In the end, the more value that can be created from such an acquisition, the better it is for everyone.

- **Technology:** IT and development environments are both important. Merging two operations should result in a reduction of systems used, but most of the time you end up with all the systems at first. Trying to get recently merged organizations to function as a single system can be difficult, but it's important to have such collaboration. Using more than one system is a disaster in all areas (reporting, employee retention, costs). So, look for, and if necessary, manufacture, ways to consolidate and simplify technology. This will save you money and keep staff from growing frustrated. Developing strong working environments is even more important. We want product teams working together as quickly as possible. If your products are built on different stacks, how those products will interoperate must be taken seriously. Plan for migrations and rewrites if required. Bite the bullet quickly to consolidate systems and technologies.

- **Culture:** Business culture encompasses the shared behaviors, procedures, values, and mindset of those working in, or with, a company or organization. It includes policies, procedures, and accepted social norms among various aspects of group dynamics. When two companies combine, so do their cultures. One culture never dominates the other completely. There is usually a new culture that needs defining with eyes wide open. There are many questions that need to be answered, such as: How are decisions made? Is data management taken seriously? Do we expect to run our business on best practices? Even questions of logistics will factor into the culture of the company, such as remote work scheduling. Leaders play a key role in merging cultures. They must set the tone in motion by demonstrating appropriate actions in public to set norms. A successful acquisition involves successful culture reinvention, so make a plan, and most importantly, work closely with your new partners on creating a culture that works for everyone involved.

There are various levels of operating leverage that may be obtained post-acquisition that can flow into the valuation. When thinking about synergies, consider the benefits that come from combining startups and resources with your potential acquirers.

- Is the acquirer contracted with any vendors that can lower operational costs?
- Are there potential up-sell or cross-sell opportunities with other startups or startup units?
- Do you have any partner relationships that would be appealing to the acquirer?

If you're a fan of classic romantic comedies—and hey, who isn't?—then you'll know that a big part of their charm is the simple, predictable formula they follow. First comes the meet cute (a movie/television term for an amusing or charming first encounter) where two people, who were obviously made for each other, are thrown together without any real effort of their own. The newly formed couple bickers and flirts, then—after a few easily resolved conflicts—profess their love, smooch, and wander off into the sunset as the credits roll.

From the outside, the acquisition process can look a bit like a love story. We focus our attention on the end result—the big, lucrative exit—and assume that the rest of the process happens more or less organically: you stumble across the perfect acquirer for your startup, sparks fly, and you seal the deal. It's straightforward, glamorous, and romantic—the kind of boardroom love story designed to get any founder's pulse racing.

Well, I'm here to tell you that, if you want a successful exit, the first thing you need to do is to take those romantic preconceptions, and, just like in the movies, you can write them on a piece of paper and throw them in a fire. The truth is that there are no easily resolved conflicts, nor a guarantee of a happy ending, which is 99 percent assured in romantic comedies. When it comes to selling, you can't just sit around waiting for

Mr. or Ms. Right to show up to acquire your startup. To get to the exit you deserve, you need to get serious, stop daydreaming, and take charge of the situation.

The Power of Partnerships to Create Acquisitions

You can't limit yourself to simply talking, of course. My best deals are struck by startups that make a point of building active partnerships with their target acquirers—something that lets you understand and build closer alignment with their needs, while giving them a closer look at your product, your customers, and the way you operate.

One of my proudest moments as a cofounder was when I sold a startup that created super-bright 900-lumen headlamps for hobby cyclists and law enforcement cyclists. (To give you an idea of just how bright that is, a flashlight you can comfortably read a book by is about 20 lumens.) What started as a quirky niche product had grown into a highly successful brand, in large part because we'd been discovered by police, who'd started adding our lamps to their standard bicycle equipment.

We were chugging along nicely, selling about 250,000 lamps per month, when my startup partner, best friend, and co-CEO passed away suddenly. I wanted to do right by his widow, so I went to the manufacturer we'd been working with for years, and one of our ideal acquirers, and convinced them they could do very well for themselves if they took our proven concept and bought the startup as a turnkey solution for going direct to the customer.

In the end, they bought the business: lock, stock, and barrel. Nothing can compensate for the loss of a spouse, but by leveraging the power of partnerships, I was able to help my best friend's grieving widow through a very difficult time.

From Investor to Acquirer

It's important to listen closely to acquirers and think about their concerns and their risks. They are often wondering: *How do I know my customers will buy this product? How do I know if the technology, product process, or whatever will seamlessly work with my current operations? How will I know if our cultures and senior leadership team will blend well?* Too often founders are focused so closely on their own concerns that they forget their acquirer has concerns of their own.

I recently went to a family wedding, and I was watching two families meet face-to-face for the first time. As you probably know, I am always thinking about startups, so I couldn't help thinking this is just like the risk acquirers take. The bet is that the two companies seamlessly integrate, everyone gets along, and two plus two becomes one hundred. This is a process that takes time; after all, we are humans. So, start early and I promise you will not be sorry you did.

When I made the investment into a public-transit startup, they already had a pretty clear idea of who their potential acquirers were. After all, they were building ticketing technology for buses, and there are only so many players in that space. As vertical subject matter experts, they'd already done a great job of reaching out to their primary ideal acquirer, and they'd built a startup that aligned with their needs.

To pave the way for an exit, the public-transit startup had developed a relationship with their ideal acquirer and proposed a partnership to co-sell touchless ticketing to public-transit agencies, along with the acquirer's end-to-end products. The acquirer loved the idea, and the two companies' co-selling projects proved a massive hit.

Next step—propose an acquisition, right? Actually, not so fast. Once we got the acquirers on the hook with a partnership deal, I told the public-transit startup crew to propose a new fundraising round of $1M or $1.5M.

I'm no fan of raising more money than you really need, but this is the one exception that proves the rule: when you're gearing up to sell, it's almost always a good idea to do a small fundraising round, and to bring your potential acquirer in as an investor. I've had the potential acquirer do a round of funding, which has given them a first right of first refusal—they can buy the company if they want or pass on the company, and the money that they gave you would be used as a deposit if they choose to buy the company. So, in those initial conversations, the best investor is going to be a potential acquirer—this way they are already putting some skin in the game.

It also provides you with an opportunity to include language in their contract as an investor that gives the acquirer an opportunity, with a deadline, and you can put in place a pre-negotiated price based on agreed multiples. Also, it plants a seed that you can nurture and a mindset that preloads some of the real diligence questions that don't come up unless you use this process, which gives you time to manage the findings without risking the exit. So now, if you prove yourself, all they have to do is exercise the option.

Acquirers have the fear of missing out, and may make offers, since you should have checked all the boxes (diligence, product, culture, customers, etc.) and now be set up really well for a negotiation. Competition is usually gnarly at that level, and if an acquirer knows their competitor is looking for a startup like yours, it is almost guaranteed that they will make an offer. If they don't, you restructure their investment as a loan or investment. The whole time, your other potential acquirers are told, "Sorry, we have a deal on the table." This also makes the whole deal look juicier to other companies and will often speed up the deal process with the acquirer/investor.

Appropriately including the right kind of language in an investment agreement lets you gauge how serious your acquirer really is. If they're willing to make an investment, but balk at the right-to-buy language, then at least you know where you stand, and you can move on quickly. On the other hand, if they make an investment on the terms you suggest, you'll know they're serious.

In the public-transit startup's case, the acquirer was enthusiastic about investing, and didn't have any concerns about the drag-along clause we proposed. "You've got them on the hook," I told the public-transit startup founders over scotch and cigars, as we lounged near a koi pond at a swanky cigar shop in San Diego. "You've made it! Get ready to have your lives changed, because we're about to get the exit you've been waiting for."

Sure enough, a few months later, the company was acquired for a cool $40M+—enough to net me and other investors a sizable return on our investments, and to ensure the public-transit startup founders would wake up wealthy the next morning and never need to ride the bus again.

Keep Your Investors at Arm's Length

These days, I'm an investor, and naturally, I'm convinced my sage words of wisdom are invaluable to the founders with whom I work. Often, as with the public-transit startup, I'm able to help them with potential acquirers.

But despite that, it's important to remember, as a founder, you should ensure your investors have the appropriate level of information as you move toward an exit. Above all, you shouldn't let your investors wade into the deal too deeply, or too early. In nearly every circumstance, founders should be careful about letting investors interact directly with your potential acquirer.

That might sound counterintuitive. After all, nobody is more invested than your investors in seeing you make it over the line and secure a big exit. In fact, this final stretch—when you're talking to a potential acquirer and moving toward an exit—is really the one time when you take into consideration all of the advice you obtain. But, at the end of the day, it is primarily your decision. The acquirer is buying a business you built, not your investors. Remember, this is your big moment, and after the exit, most often, you will be required to stay on after the transaction, but your investors will be on to their next deals.

After I had started talks with a buyer for a magazine startup I had built, I had a potential acquirer sniffing around and kicking the tires on our startup. Unfortunately, though, I touted the situation to my investors too early, when I wasn't ready to make any decisions. My investors didn't say anything bad about the startup, of course—quite the contrary! They came out, guns blazing, and gave the most aggressive, upbeat pitch possible for our startup, trying to drive up the value of the deal.

That might sound like a good thing, but it meant that, for our potential acquirer, the only way to go was down. As they looked more closely at our startup, they inevitably found areas where we weren't perfectly aligned with their needs—and because they'd been told we were God's gift to our industry, they went away disappointed, and it became hard to rev up their enthusiasm again.

It is important to keep investors in the right mindset, along with yourself. For example, I could have told my target acquirer early on about the areas where they might have concerns, then progressively gotten them more and more excited as they learned more about the way our startup *did* match their needs. But because my investors weighed in and over-egged things early on, I lost control of the conversation, and ultimately the deal fell through.

The bottom line is that, while investors are incredibly important partners as you build your startup, when the time comes to sell, *you* need to be the one driving the bus. Earlier, we talked about having a narrative. Here, too, you need to construct your own narrative of what you want to tell your potential acquirers and how and when you want to provide more specifics. Investors need to be willing to sit back and trust the CEO they've invested in, and as a founder, you need to have the gumption to push back and tell your investors to take a back seat when necessary. Nobody understands your startup or its value better than you, so don't let your investors get underfoot, even if they mean well, when you're trying to cement your exit.

Get the Best Deal at the Right Time

Of course, when you're cementing an acquisition deal, you want to get the best price you can for your startup. But the reality is that your acquirer will usually have a pretty clear formula—such as a certain multiple of your bottom-line or top-line revenues and a priority of value drivers, like synergies, growth, margin, and retention—that they use to determine what they're willing to pay for a startup.

You do have some wiggle room when you're negotiating with your acquirer. But getting a good price doesn't just mean demanding tens of millions of dollars with a straight face; it means being able to show clear reasons why your startup is worth more than their established framework would suggest. That's partly why it's so important to do a good job of identifying your synergies, like your ICP, early on. The more you can show that your startup aligns squarely with your acquirer, the easier it will be to negotiate a higher acquisition price. Things like standardization, systems, processes, performance metrics, and KPIs can demand a premium, and automation and your optimization efforts will show the ability to scale. In fact, I have experienced this more than once and actually was told by an acquirer, "I want the minnow to swallow the whale."

Ultimately, all these steps will spell less risk, which means more value and leverage. Such negotiations come down to risk and opportunity. The acquirer wants to know what their potential upside is, and what level of risk they're taking on by purchasing your startup. Your track record (probability and predictability), such as your lagging and leading indicators, will be invaluable to the advisory board at this phase (Exit). This is why you need to document all the decisions you've made along the way, and also show the processes and best practices you've developed as you've grown your startup.

This is also part of the reason that building partnerships with acquirers is so important. It allows you to de-risk their calculations by proving that you can integrate with their company and to goose the upside by proving you can create real value for them.

Before selling Affiliate Traction, for instance, I partnered with an eBay company and showed that I was able to put together a technical integration to send clients into their system. As a result, when we negotiated the acquisition, I was able to show them clearly not just that my customers were a perfect match for their ideal customer profile, but that I knew how to seamlessly move my customers across to them. That means my acquirer would immediately start receiving all the software and service fees my customers were paying, along with the other revenues they brought in— and that, in turn, allowed me to argue for a higher multiple.

Never Say Never

Of course, not every deal works out. Even my most successful startups didn't sell to the first acquirers I pitched them to. In my case, that was because those startups were not fully complete, and didn't have a clear framework to guide my progress toward an exit. Even if you do everything right, you'll find that not every potential acquisition will result in a successful exit. Inevitably, some deals simply won't pan out.

That's actually by design. When you use the Startup Science Lifestyle system, you start looking for potential acquirers early on as you complete your ecosystem and North Star. But you don't just find *one* potential acquirer—instead, you identify a number of businesses that could potentially buy your startup. Over time, you'll focus more clearly on a handful of those acquirers—based on opportunities you see, relationships you build, and your ability to create alignment—and you'll let the others fall by the wayside. As your startup evolves, dropping some potential acquirers lets you focus more intently on the ones with the biggest potential upside.

Crucially, though, you should never say never when it comes to an acquisition. I always tell founders that, until the ink is dry on the contract and they've received the funds, they should keep on talking to other potential acquirers and maintaining the relationships they've built, even if they are no longer actively tailoring the startup to their needs. I have a friend who is an experienced startup founder, who had a company lined up to be acquired by Silicon Valley Bank, which was, arguably, one of the most stable acquires at the time, then *boom*! You know what happened. Overnight, they went from a big success to laying off just about everyone and having to pivot completely. After a lunch, I could hear the pain in their voices and see the pain on their faces, but I just had to ask, what about other acquisition partners? They had built the company and focused on a single acquirer, and when that fell through, they had no backup plan. This could have been avoided. What's worse, guess who gave them that advice? Yes, investors and the board. Never ever count on a transaction before you check your account and see the zeros and the commas.

Some deals do fall through, even at the last minute, and for that reason, you might need a plan B. Having options is also the best way to project success and drive up the value of your eventual exit. If your acquirer knows you're chatting with one or two of their rivals, your value will only climb—because even if you're mostly chatting about the weather, your acquirer will assume you're close to finalizing an acquisition and will raise their own valuation of your startup accordingly.

The bottom line is that the acquisition process is exactly that, a *process*. You need to keep that process running in parallel for two or more potential buyers, even if you think you've found your ideal acquirer and you're ready to ditch the rest. Ultimately, keeping your eventual buyer hungry and a little bit nervous until the deal is signed is the best way to ensure you get what your startup is truly worth.

Don't Quit

When my first Affiliate Traction deal fell through, I spent a while wallowing in depression. So much wasted time! So much wasted effort! And a multimillion-dollar deal I'd never see again! But after a day or two, I looked in the mirror and staged an intervention for myself. "Okay, Greg, you messed that up," I told myself. "And okay, yes, this sucks. But, at the same time, now you know how it works—and you aren't going to make this mistake again."

I took some comfort in that. I've always believed that what doesn't kill you makes you stronger, and hey, I wasn't dead yet. So, I picked myself up and went back to work.

It took me several long years to rebuild my startup and implement the hard-won lessons I had learned. But in the end, by keeping my target acquirers front-of-mind while I restructured, I was able to secure an exit that made everyone—me, my investors, and the acquirer—very happy indeed.

The reality is that finding the right acquirer isn't some mysterious process in which fate brings you and your one perfect match together. This isn't a rom-com. There are no meet cutes, and you won't find your acquirer simply by locking eyes with them across a crowded room or even swiping left or right on a website. Instead, you need to plan ahead, put the work in, and keep on showing up until you get the results you want.

The whole point of StartupScience.io, in fact, is to *remove* that sense of romance and mystery from the process of building a startup. If you've learned anything over the past 200+ pages, I hope it's that building a startup is a process that you can approach scientifically and succeed at by following a clear and methodical process.

That might sound a bit less glamorous or exciting than you were hoping for, but I hope it also feels empowering. You don't have to wait for the stars to align, or simply hope and wait for your acquirer to find you. Armed with what you've learned in these pages, and what you can unlock as you dig deeper into StartupScience.io, you'll find it's possible to grow a startup, avoid the pitfalls that sink so many startups, and chart a course forward. You now have the power to make it happen, so buckle up and keep on pushing your startup forward until you win the exit!

CHAPTER WRAP-UP

StartupScience.io is designed to help founders achieve a well-priced and well-timed exit. Achieving objectives at each phase creates the best opportunity for you (the founder) to achieve that well-priced exit. Use your ecosystem map to find potential acquirers and partner with them. Manage against your valuation drivers to increase the value of your exit. Keep going, don't quit, and you can create meaningful wealth for yourself and your community.

Use this QR code for finding the right buyer.

Conclusion

It is not the critic who counts; not the person who points out how the strong person stumbles, or where the doer of deeds could have done them better. The credit belongs to the person who is actually in the arena, whose face is marred by dust and sweat and blood; who strives valiantly; who errs, who comes short again and again, because there is no effort without error and shortcoming; but who does actually strive to do the deeds; who knows great enthusiasms, the great devotions; who spends themselves in a worthy cause; who at the best knows in the end the triumph of high achievement, and who at the worst, if they fail, at least fails while daring greatly, so that their place shall never be with those cold and timid souls who neither know victory nor defeat.

–Theodore Roosevelt

H. L. Hunt, the legendary Texas oil tycoon, knew a thing or two about money. After losing his shirt betting on cotton futures, Hunt rebuilt his fortune playing five-card stud, according to legend. He won his first oil well on the turn of a card, and routinely used his poker winnings to pay the wages of his drilling crews. After buying up oil claims in Arkansas, Texas, Canada, and Libya, he accumulated a monumental fortune. By the time he died in 1974, he was believed to be the richest man in the world.

Still, old H. L. had a pretty relaxed attitude toward his wealth. "You can only sleep in one bed at a time. You can only wear one suit at a time. You can only drive one automobile at a time. And you can only eat one meal at a time," he used to say. "If you've made a lot of money, it's really just a matter of keeping score."

I found myself thinking back on Hunt's words when I made my first big exit. I'd left my lawyer's office in something of a daze, and after a celebratory smoke or two, I realized I was exhausted and stumbled off to bed. A few hours later, though, I suddenly sat bolt upright and reached for my laptop.

Sitting there in the dark, the blue light from the screen glowing on my face, I checked my bank balance. The deposit had cleared, and suddenly, there was more money than I'd ever seen in my life sitting in my account. True, I still wasn't operating at H. L. Hunt's level, but by any objective standard, I had suddenly become wealthy. If money was about keeping score, then I'd hit the net.

Weirdly, though, I didn't feel like a winner. In fact, when I woke up the next morning, the whole thing felt like a dream. I checked my account again in the light of day; the money was still sitting there. But it didn't feel real. I felt like a bank error had been made in my favor and that, at any moment, someone would realize it and take the money away.

It wasn't until a week or two later that the imposter syndrome started to subside, and I realized my life had changed. Gradually, I forced myself to start buying things. I bought my wonderful, long-suffering wife a Range Rover. We bought a bigger house and paid off debts. We spread the wealth around too. I bought my brother a tractor and trailer he needed for his construction startup. I bought a franchise for my sister. I was able to help my mom with some projects on the home and land where we grew up, in tents, as kids, and we launched our own philanthropic fund to support a long list of causes that mattered to us.

I've seen other founders go through the same process of disbelief, followed by gradual realization that their lives have been changed forever. After their exit, my friends at the public-transit startup went from being in debt to having wealth that would keep them and their families comfortable for the rest of their lives. I'm not saying this to brag, but because it's what I want for you too.

If you follow the steps outlined in this book, you'll be in a place to change your life for the better. What you do with that is up to you, but the point is that you'll be free to write your own rules, and play the game on your own terms. Strip away the anxieties that come with *not* having money, and you aren't just rich; you're free to spend your life doing whatever you feel truly matters to you—you are wealthy. That's an amazing gift, and it's something the Startup Science Lifecycle was explicitly designed to bring within reach of as many founders as possible.

This is ultimately where H. L. Hunt and I disagree. I don't think money is simply about keeping score, and I don't think it's just something that opens the door to a pleasant life with fancy cars, fine wines, and luxury homes. The life-changing wealth you get when you make it to a successful exit is important because it gives you the ability to rewrite the rules—for yourself, and hopefully, for others—in order to follow your dreams, and hopefully make the world a better place in the process.

For me, freedom from worry meant the freedom to spend my time studying and learning and applying the things I learned to growing startups toward an exit better and faster. Every startup I've been involved with has taught me something new, and I've had the luxury of spending time digesting those lessons and distilling them into a coherent and replicable science that anyone can utilize and apply to their own startup.

By writing this book, I've tried to share those lessons with others. My hope is that by codifying and explaining the process of building a successful startup, I'll be able to reduce the number of startups that fail. That will help more people build generational wealth for themselves and their families, driving social mobility and creating enormous benefits for their communities.

If this sounds like hokum to you, that's perfectly fine. The whole point of making it in a startup is that it's given me the freedom to do what I want, and pursue the things I believe are important, regardless of whether anyone agrees with me. When you complete your own exit, you'll be free to completely ignore what I think, and do whatever you want with your life.

But I do hope that, if you follow StartupScience.io and secure a successful exit, you'll take this one piece of advice: don't assume that the exit is the finish line. It's actually just the beginning of a new phase in your life—one in which you'll have the freedom to pursue your own goals, and the means to make a difference in the world. That means your exit isn't a no-strings-attached reward for the effort you've put in. It also comes with the responsibility, and maybe even the obligation, to keep on growing and learning, and to use your position for the good of other people.

So sure, have fun with your newfound wealth. Life is short, and there's nothing wrong with enjoying yourself. But don't waste the opportunity you've been given. Don't treat money as an end in itself, and don't worry about keeping score. Just figure out what's really important to you, and use your freedom to pursue it. And if StartupScience.io has proven useful to you along the way, I hope you'll pay the debt forward—by following my mom's campsite rule and trying to leave the world a little better than you found it.

ACKNOWLEDGMENTS

Nothing is done alone, and a book is no exception. I have learned that writing a good book is a team sport. That said, please accept a heartfelt thank-you to my team, Jeremy Gordon, Marty Bickford, Jill Speckman, Gary Horn, and Michael Silverman, for their contributions. I also want to express my deepest gratitude for the support and feedback from Owen Matthews of Alacrity Canada, Robin McLay and Michael Hawes of Fulbright, and Greg Horowitt at UCSD/Stanford. I also want to thank my friend Rich Mintzer, who did an amazing job organizing, editing, and putting the book together. Finally, a huge acknowledgment to my best friend and partner in life, Lisa. Thank you for all the hours of reading, feedback, and patience. You are my rock.

ABOUT THE AUTHOR

Gregory Shepard is a twenty-year startup veteran and serial entrepreneur with twelve liquidity events under his belt, two of which were sold as part of a $925M transaction that won four private equity awards for transactions between $250M and $1B.

Gregory is an authority in the startup space, authoring over 100 articles in publications like *Forbes*, *Fortune*, *Entrepreneur*, the *New York Observer*, and the *Deal*. A startup personality appearing on TV, radio, over 100 popular podcasts, on the TEDx stage, and as a keynote speaker at Ivy League universities and conferences worldwide, his talks inspire the masses. Greg also hosts the ForbesBooks podcast *Startup Science*.

As an investor, Greg cofounded a global syndicate that focuses on series seed technology businesses that prefer operational expertise and guidance to achieve rewarding, capital-efficient outcomes. BOSS Capital Partners has had multiple technology exits from $50M up. Humble beginnings molded by struggles with neurodivergence and poverty haven't stopped Greg from becoming the successful entrepreneur, author, and philanthropist he is today.

Greg's success story of overcoming obstacles is what drives him to support young entrepreneurs looking to spark positive change in the world around them, spreading his message of "altruistic capitalism." From growing up with very little, to navigating a world not built for those with neurodivergences, Greg continues to be one of the most recognizable examples of how fearless optimism and steadfast determination can guide any intelligent and determined young professional toward success.

He lives in San Diego with his wife, two children, and his potbellied pig, Winnebago.

To learn more about StartupScience.io, check out startupscience.io:

To learn more about Greg, check out gregoryshepard.com: